Big Book of Little
BEARS

Identification & Price Guide

Brecka

Published by

krause publications

The World's Largest Hobby & Collectibles Publisher

Please, call or write us for our free catalog of antiques and collectibles publications. To place an order or receive our free catalog, call 800-258-0929. For editorial comment and further information, use our regular business telephone at (715) 445-2214.

Library of Congress Catalog Number: 99-68990
ISBN: 1-58221-021-7
Printed in the United States of America

Dedication

This book is dedicated to my daughter and husband, and my family.

Acknowledgments

Thank you to the following people for their support, feedback and help: Becky Fox, Don Gulbrandsen, Kris Manty, Andi Lucas, Allan Miller, and all the great folks at Krause Publications.

And a whole lot of appreciation to these fine and helpful people and the companies they represent for their assistance:

Grace Añonuevo at The Idea Factory (Meanies)

Lisa Behe (the Boyd's Collection ltd.)

Judy Berwick at Gund

Adam Cohen at Liquid Blue (Grateful Dead Bean Bears)

Steven Gillman at The Limited Connection, Inc. (Classy Tassy's Bears)

Kit Kiefer for Salvino's Bammers

*Stephani Perlmutter for Cavanagh Group International
(Coca-Cola Bean Bag Plush, Harley-Davidson Bean Bag Plush)*

Gary Hallett, Jennifer Swift and Darlene Kriewaldt

Preface

Did you have a bear or Teddy Bear to help you go to sleep or feel safe when you were a youngster? I did. I loved him very much, and I still have him. His name is "Beary." Today's children have many hi-tech toys to choose from, but, when it's time to go to sleep, many still reach for their stuffed bear or other soft animal (my daughter's choice is a Ty plush dog that she calls "Butterscotch").

Bears are not only a favorite among children, but they are the choice of millions of collectors worldwide. Perhaps it's the desire to regain the innocence of youth that so many people collect bears. Maybe it's because they're so darn cute!

It's nearing 100 years that the Teddy Bear has been around. Reportedly, President Theodore Roosevelt provided the inspiration for the Teddy Bear. As the story goes, Roosevelt was on a hunting trip in Mississippi when the hunting party tracked and captured a black bear and tied it to a tree for the President to shoot. Roosevelt refused to kill the bear, saying it was unsportsmanlike. The next day, an editorial cartoon immortalized the event, which sparked the idea for the Teddy Bear.

There's a lot to collect when it comes to bears, especially from the 1990s. In fact, this might be the decade of the bear! The current bear craze began with the introduction of Ty's Beanie Baby line in 1994. Most prized among the early Beanies were the colored Teddy Bears. As the beanbag market continued to develop, it became clear that bears and Teddy Bears were collectors' favorites. Ty continued to produce hot Teddy Bears like Garcia, Peace, Libearty and Princess. At the same time, Ty also produced a successful line of mostly bear characters called Attic Collectibles.

Starting in 1997 and continuing to the present, several companies have joined the beanbag bear bonanza: Grateful Dead Bean Bears, Salvino's Bammers, Limited Treasures, Classic Collecticritters, Celebrity Bears, Classy Tassy's Bears and others. In addition, several promotional, advertising and character-themed bears were made.

The Big Book of Little Bears chronicles the recent beanbag bears, as well as other popular contemporary lines of "little" bears (such as Attic Collectibles and Boyd's Bears). There's even a section for Winnie-the-Pooh! (As a bonus, I've added a cat and dog bean bag

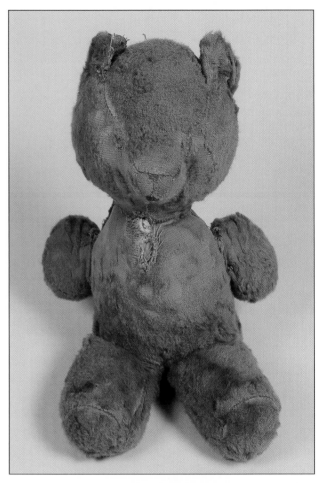

The author's childhood bear, "Beary," is now tattered and missing his eyes, but he is still much loved!

section which features what I feel are some of the best canines and felines.)

As an author, I hope this guide will assist you in building your bear collection. As a bear and Teddy Bear lover, I hope this book will make you smile and think about simpler times when you went to sleep with your favorite bear in your arms.

Have a great time collecting bears...and cats & dogs, too!

Shawn Brecka
Bean Family
P.O. Box 441
Plover, WI 54467-0441

Table of Contents

Listings, Photos & Values

The Bears

The Cats

The Dogs

Introduction

About this Guide

Collecting bears has seen a splendid revival in the 1990s with the release and subsequent rise in popularity of Ty Beanie Baby Teddy Bears. The interest in Ty's products was the fuel needed to fire-up an entire collecting area. Over the past couple of years, several bean bag bear-only companies have sprung up. In addition, longtime plush bear companies, such as Boyd's Bears, have added many collectors to their products.

The Big Book of Little Bears is a full-color price and identification guide featuring collectible bears from the 1990s to the present (as well as cats and dogs). It includes all types of bears: Teddys, pandas, koalas, cartoon bears, real bears, advertising bears and so on. Right now there's as good of a selection as ever for bear collectors. I fully expect a bullish market in bean bag and plush bear market well into the new century.

Bear Trends

Trend #1: Collectors specialize. One trend I've noticed is that there are so many different bear lines to choose from that collectors are now beginning specialize in a few bear areas. It's hard enough to keep up with three or four lines of bears, let alone dozens. I go by the adage of "collect what you like and you won't be disappointed."

Trend #2: Overproduction. You could say that bears are breeding like rabbits. Companies need to adjust their production levels to more closely match demand. What that likely means is lower production runs to retain collectibility levels. If sellers are "blowing out" bears at close to wholesale prices because they have too many in stock, it does not bode well for those companies' products, no matter how well they're made.

Trend #3: Promotional and advertising bears. These types of bears are gaining a niche in the hobby, as they are generally produced in smaller quantities, and they often feature a mascot bear that appeals to collectors outside the hobby (i.e., the A&W Bear and the Teddy Grahams Teddy Bears).

Tips for Buying & Selling Bears

Buying bears: Start at the retail level to find what you're looking for, whether it's a Beanie Baby retailer, Disney venue, Warner Brothers Studio Store, etc. For retired, discontinued and regional bears, look for other collectors or dealers from across the country (and even

Creative Memories promotional bear "Scrappie" is very hard to find and in high demand.

as far away as Japan, England and Australia). I've done most of my buying via the Internet. Bean bag and bear shows are great places to find items you're looking for. Magazines, such as Toy Shop and Beans! Magazine have many ads for bears.

Selling bears: If you sell bears in-person, the sale is pretty straight forward. If you sell through the mail (Internet or magazines), make sure you describe the bear with complete accuracy, especially condition of the bear and the tags. If you sell to a dealer, expect offers anywhere from 25% to 75% of the values quoted in price guides. Obviously, selling bears yourself, when you become the "dealer," is the best way to get the best price. Becoming a part-time seller, to help supplement your pocketbook for collecting, has become a lot easier with the advent of the Internet.

Buying on the Internet: Don't let the Internet scare you. I've had very few problems buying bears on the Internet. While there are Internet rip-off artists, there are ways to protect yourself when buying on-line. I've purchased bears from individuals, companies and through on-line auctions. If buying from an individual or company, check their references. Don't give out your credit card number unless you're 100% positive of the legitimacy of the seller, and then only through a secure server (one that makes it virtually impossible for others to tap into your message and swipe your credit card number). If the seller accepts credit cards, it's just as simple to make a phone call to place your order. One of the hottest auction sites on the Internet for buying and selling bears is eBay at www.ebay.com. Don't jump in with both feet either buying or selling. Get some experience and understand how buying and selling works on-line.

Doing Business on eBay

While there are other auction services on-line, nothing beats eBay for sheer number and variety of bears. To use this auction site, go to www.ebay.com and become a registered user (it's free, and there are easy-to-follow instructions at the site). After that, you can bid on items and put items up for auction. One of the main fears people have about bidding on auctions is the trustworthiness of the sellers. While not foolproof, eBay is almost self-policing. As registered users on eBay buy and sell items, those they have done business with leave feedback that for the user. If you're bidding on an item from a seller with a positive "feedback" rating of 100, with no negative comments, feel pretty confident that you'll have a good experience buying from that person. I very rarely bid on items from sellers with very low feedback ratings (below 5) or those with several negative feedbacks in proportion to positive feedbacks. Oftentimes, you'll find someone with a very high rating who has few negative feedbacks; even excellent sellers will run across a "loose cannon" now and then.

Tips for buying on eBay

1. The heaviest bidding usually occurs in the final 30 minutes of the auction. To get the best price, I try to bid in the last five minutes or so. Sometimes you win, sometimes you lose. Other people are doing the same thing you're doing.

2. Don't be the first kid on the block to buy a bear. The first auctions of a new bear will almost always be very inflated. Exert patience and wait until prices come down to more reasonable levels. You don't want to be holding a bear you paid $200 for, only to find it at a later date for $10.

3. It's fun to bid on and win items, but be sure you intend to actually purchase what you're bidding on. Don't get caught up in how much fun it is to bid, only

to realize that your eyes were bigger than your pocketbook. If you don't honor your bid, it's likely the seller will give you a negative "feedback" comment. Too many negative feedbacks rightfully spell d-o-o-m.

4. Bidding wars. It's happened to me. To beat a competitor who had been outbidding me all night, I bid much higher than I originally intended. I won the item, but I lost the war. Set a maximum limit and don't go past it. Remember that the item you're bidding on will likely be offered again by other sellers.

5. When the seller emails you, write him/her back as soon as possible. Include your name, address and other pertinent details or special requests.

6. If you want your package insured, tell the seller and include the extra money for the insurance. I generally insure the more expensive items I buy. Priority mail shipping through the U.S. Postal Service seems to be the least expensive way and the preferred shipping method of Internet sellers. Because of most bears' size and weight, $3.20 is the usual charge.

7. I generally send a money order, as this helps ensure a quick turnaround of the package. If it's an item you're not concerned about getting quickly and the seller accepts personal checks, you can save yourself a little money by sending a personal check vs. buying a money order. You can send cash. I don't recommended it, but I will send cash sometimes if the amount is less than $5 or $10.

8 Tips for selling on eBay

1. It doesn't seem to matter too much what day your auctions end. The only advice is to not have them end in the very late hours of the night or the wee hours of the morning.

2. If you can, include a picture of the item you're selling. Pictures add money to the bids you'll receive. There's something comforting in bidders' minds about actually seeing the item they're bidding on. It's also good if you're trying to show the condition of tags. A picture is worth a thousand words.

3. Fully describe your item and its condition. Don't try to hide the warts. If a tag has problems, describe them. That way, the buyer will know what he or she is getting and the chance that an item will be returned are greatly reduced. Fully spell out the type of shipping (i.e., first class, priority, etc.) and the charges for shipping. I don't bid on items where the seller adds a large "handling" fee. Also, state the type of payment you'll accept and how quickly you will ship the item once the payment is received.

4. eBay allows you to set a minimum bid and/or a reserve price. If you have a bean bag that you want to

get $30 for, set your minimum bid or a reserve at that price. If the bidder doesn't reach that price, you are not obligated to sell the bidder the item, nor is the bidder obligated to buy the item. If it turns out you later decide you'd be willing to sell the item for less than what you placed your reserve at, contact the high bidder, as many times the high bidder will agree to purchase.

5. When the auction is complete, e-mail the winner as soon as possible, with the auction number, name of item, the winning bid amount, postage and/or insurance cost and a total cost. Also, include the address you'd like the check or money order sent to. Here's an example of an effective e-mail letter:

Thanks for your winning bids on the following:

1. Erin Beanie Baby, Auction No. 0000000000, $7.00
2. Osito Beanie Baby, Auction No. 0000000000, $12.00

With $3.20 for priority shipping, your total is $22.50. Insurance is at your option for 85 cents extra. You can pay by check (wait to clear) or money order (immediate shipping). Send money to:

John Doe
460 Elm Street
Anywhere, USA 00000

P.S.: Send me your name and address so I can get your package ready to ship.

6. Many sellers will take nothing but money orders, cashier's checks and so on, and don't accept personal checks. If you accept personal checks, allow time for the check to clear your bank before you send the buyer the item. Tell the buyer in your first e-mail, "money orders shipped the next day, personal checks will wait 10 days before shipping" or whatever is appropriate.

7. Sometimes, buyers forget to send their money or thought they did when they didn't. This has even happened to me once or twice, especially if I bought a whole bunch of items at the same time. It can get confusing. A gentle e-mail reminder is usually enough to prompt action from the buyer.

8. If a bidder reneges on a bid (I've had this happen a couple of times), I leave the bidder negative feedback. It would have to be a really, really good and believable reason for me not to leave negative feedback. This is the way the Internet auction system polices itself. Leaving a negative comment isn't a pleasant thing to do, but it's the way it makes the whole process work as well as it does.

As I said, take time to learn to properly do business on eBay and you will have a positive experience.

Learn the Lingo

What follows are lists of commonly used terms and abbreviations:

Terms

Common: A bear that is easily found through usual retail outlets for retail price.

Current: A bear that is in production and available for sale at retail stores.

Discontinued: A bear style or version that is no longer in production but has not been officially retired by the company.

Exclusive: A bear that is available only through select venues. Coca-Cola has several exclusive bear offerings.

Generation (1st, 2nd, 3rd, etc.): Refers to the style of tag used. Also known as "tag style."

Hang tag: The tag that is attached to the bear by a plastic tag fastener or elastic (such as on the Grateful Dead Bean Bears).

Holiday bear: A special bear made for the holiday season. These bean bags are usually available only during the particular holiday season.

Limited edition: A bear that is produced for a certain holiday, period of time or in limited, predetermined quantities.

Loved: Refers to a bear that has been played with and shows signs of wear.

Manufacturing oddity: A bear with an error, such as a missing patch, that happened during the manufacturing process.

Mistake: A bear with a mistake such as incorrect tush tags.

New release: A bear that is the most recent new release by a company.

Promotional: A bear that is used to promote a company's product(s). Also known as "Advertising."

Rare: Often abused term to describe the availability of a bear. Rare should imply that a bear is hard to find and that only a few exist. More often, the correct term should be "scarce." For instance, people said that the Beanie Baby Princess was rare, which was not true. It was scarce at first because there weren't enough to satisfy demand.

Retired: A bear that is no longer in production, but may still be available at the retail level for retail price.

Scarce: Implies that a bear is hard to find, but there are several examples in existence. In bear terms, "scarce" usually means that an item has just been released and only a small percentage of collectors/dealers have gotten their hands on the bear. "Scarce" bears usually wind up being common.

Style change: A change made to an existing bear resulting in a new look for the bear, such as a change in the material used or an item added like a white star or black paws.

Tag protector: A plastic or acrylic device placed around or on the hang tag to protect it.

Tush tag: The sewn-in tag on a bear that usually contains manufacturing information and the like.

Variation: A bear that was issued in one particular style and consequently changed, such as a star added or a color changed.

Abbreviations

1G, 2G, 3G, etc.: First generation, second generation, third generation hang tags

BBs: Beanie Babies

CC: Credit card

CDN: Canadian

DL: Disneyland

DS: Disney Store

HTF: Hard to find

MBBP: Mini Bean Bag Plush (proper name for Disney bean bags)

MIB: Mint in bag, mint in box or mint in blister

MIP: Mint in package

MKT: Mouseketoys

MWBMT: Mint with both mint tags

MWMT: Mint with mint tags

MWT: Mint with tag (tag is not mint)

NF: New face (Beanie Baby Teddy)

NM: Near mint (condition)

NR: New release or ("no reserve" on Internet auctions, also "no res")

OF: Old face (Beanie Baby Teddy)

OT: Old tag

PE: Polyethylene (type of plastic pellets used in bears)

PVC: Polyvinyl Chloride (type of plastic pellets used in bears)

Ret'd or Ret: Retired

S/H: Shipping and handling

TBB: Teenie Beanie Babies

V1, V2, V3, etc.: Version 1, Version 2, Version 3

VHTF: Very hard to find

WB: Warner Brothers

WDW: Walt Disney World

Displaying & Taking Care of Your Bears

For display, shelves, baskets and cases work well. If you want to keep your bears from the everyday dust, buy a display case. The case protects your bears from dust and cats and kids, and it is an excellent way to showcase your collection. You can also buy individual plastic cases to hold your more valuable bears. They cost from $2-$4 each, but are worth it for your more expensive bears. For bears that I don't display, I pack them in air-tight plastic zipper-style bags inside plastic tubs.

Don't forget to use hang-tag protectors. There are tag protectors in every shape and size to fit just about any bear on the market. Protecting tags is well worth the cost, as 25% to 50% of the value of a bear is in the tag. Sometimes, however, especially with Ty Attics, there is not enough space to put a tag protector on, and you can cause more damage to the tag by putting a protector on than just leaving it as it is.

If your collection is valuable, insure the bears. Take pictures and keep an inventory of your collection. You can use your camcorder to videotape your collection. Put your photos/VCR tape and inventory list in a safety deposit box or another secure area away from your home. You never know when your collection could be stolen or lost in a natural disaster or fire. Visual proof of your collection will make life a lot easier if you have to file an insurance claim.

About the Values in this Guide

The values for the bears (and the cats and dogs) in this guide have been arrived at through various collectors' and dealers' sales lists, Internet auction results and input from various experts from across the United States. The prices are average secondary market ranges for mint bears. This price is what you can expect to pay for a bear from a seller.

The values in this book should be used only as a guide. In the near future, prices for some of the bears in the book will increase far above the listed values, due to retirements, style changes and other unpredictable factors. Prices for some bears might decrease. Keep these things in mind when using this guide. An (R) proceeding a listing refers to a bear that is known to be retired.

How Condition Affects Value

Hang Tags

Like it or not, your bears' hang tags have about 50% to do with their values. The tush tags are not nearly as important as the hang tags. It's important that the proper tush tags are in place, but their condition has little to do with overall values. Here are some general condition factors for tags and how they affect bear prices:

Mint: A perfect tag without creases, scratches, dings or dents; and no price sticker or sticker residue (if your bear has a price sticker, my advice is to leave it on, since you'll likely cause more damage trying to take it off). The prices in this guide are for bears with mint tags. As general rule, the bigger and flimsier the tag, the more likely the tag is going to have some bends or creases or other problem.

Near Mint: An almost perfect tag. Often, what makes a mint tag a near mint tag is a bend, nick or dent, but no creases. A mint tag with a price sticker on it would fall in the near mint category. Valued at 80% to 90% of the mint price.

Excellent: This tag might have a slight crease and a few other minor problems. Valued at 65% to 75% of the mint price.

Very Good: May have large creases, dents or dings, but it is still a complete hang tag that is displayable and presentable. Valued at 50% to 60% of the mint price.

Less than Very Good: A tag with many problems, including writing on the inside or back of the tag.

These are just general guidelines, but this does make you appreciate the value of sinking a few bucks into getting the proper tag protectors. Many hang tags will fall in-between the above conditions. For instance, a perfect hang tag with the price written on the back in marker, is not a mint tag nor is it a low-grade tag. It falls somewhere in the middle of the condition scale. Don't pay top price for a tag that is in less than top condition.

The Bear

There isn't much leeway when it comes to bear condition. Either the bear is in mint, unplayed-with condition, or it's in played-with condition. If you have mint bear without tags, the value is 35% to 50% a the same bear with mint tags. A played-with bear, depending on the amount of wear, could be valued from 10% to 25% of a mint bear with mint tags.

Another factor to consider is dirt and dust, which is especially bad when it comes to light-colored bears. Keep the white bears away from dust. Finally, sometimes the bears aren't mint when they arrive from the factories. Poor stitching is a common complaint. If a bear has some factory errors, it is not considered mint.

Counterfeit Beanie Baby Bears

A new market has developed for counterfeit, or "fake" Beanie Babies. So far, this doesn't seem to have happened with other brands of bears. As a bear escalates in value, so does the desire of crooks to make counterfeits to swindle unsuspecting consumers. Protecting yourself is of the utmost importance, especially if you are planning on paying big money for a hard-to-find retired Beanie Baby bear. Some things that have been noted about counterfeit beanies are poor quality stitching, smudged or poorly printed writing on tags, gold flaking on or uneven gold around the Ty heart hang tag. Often, the Beanie is very under-stuffed.

Make sure that you are buying your Beanies from an authorized Ty dealer (one that sells them at the suggested retail price) or a reputable secondary-market dealer. The best thing to do if you are unsure of the authenticity of a particular Beanie Baby is to compare it to one you are sure is real. Even then, it may be difficult to see the differences. As the counterfeiters become more sophisticated, it will become increasingly hard to ascertain fakes from the real thing. Here are some questions to ask when comparing an authentic Beanie Baby and a suspect Beanie:

1. Look at small details, such as ears, eyes and appendages. Are they the same shape, size and color?

2. Are materials the same color, feel and quality?

3. Are tush tags the same? (check size, ink color, smudging, spelling, font used)

4. Are the hang tags a match? (check the gold foil, spelling, smoothness, color of ink, fonts used)

Great Bear Resources

Throughout the book, where applicable, I have included addresses (both Internet and actual addresses) and/or phone numbers of places you can find those particular bears (and cats and dogs). Here are a few Internet sites that I regularly use to find out about new bears:

The Disney Beanie Report: *www.dizbeanies.com*
Ty official site: *www.ty.com*
Tracey's Collectibles and Gifts:
    members.tripod.com/~tracysgifts/collectibles.html
eBay auction site: *www.ebay.com*
Bugsbeanies: *www.bugsbeanies.com*
Scooby's Beanie Shack:
    looneytunes.acmecity.com/tweety/213/
BeanieMom's NetLetter: *www.beaniemom.com*
Beans! & Bears Magazine:
    www.beansmagazine.com/index.html

The
Bears

1997 A&W Bear.

A&W Bear

Two versions of this advertising bear have been issued so far, in 1997 and in 1998. They were both available for sale at A&W Restaurants across the country.

Bear	**Price Range**
1997 A&W Bear, orange shirt and hat (R) . . . .$10-$12	
1998 A&W Bear, teal shirt and hat (R) . . . .$6-$8	

Anaheim Mighty Ducks Booster Club Bear.

Anaheim Mighty Ducks Booster Club Bear

This white hockey bean bag bear was reportedly produced in a quantity of just 2,000. He was made available to members of the Mighty Ducks Booster Club on March 17, 1999. On his front is "Mighty Ducks Booster Club" and on his back is embroidered "Booster 1999." He is available only through secondary-market resources.

Bear	Price Range
Anaheim Mighty Ducks Booster Club Bear (R)	$18-$25

Australian Football League Brisbane Lions.

Australian Football League

From my source "down under," I found out about these Australian Football League (Australian Rules Football) bears. Each is the same bear, only with the shirt of its respective team. These sell for about $8 each. Teams include: Adelaide Crows, Brisbane Lions, Carlton Blues, Collingwood Magpies, Essendon Bombers, Fremantle Dockers, Geelong Cats, Hawthorn Hawks, Melbourne Demons, North Melbourne Kangaroos, Port Adelaide, Richmond Tigers, St. Kilda Saints, Sydney Swans, West Coast Eagles, Western Bulldogs.

Avon

So far, Avon has issued two Full O' Beans sets, each with one bear. The first set was retired some time ago and you'll have to find the bear on the secondary market. Check with your Avon representative to see if the 1999 bear is yet available.

Bear	Price Range
Full O' Beans Set #1, 1998 (R)	
Bernard the Bear ....$8-$10	
Full O' Beans Set #2, 1999 (Birthstone)	
February/Cody the Bear (amethyst) ....$6-$8	

Above: Cody the Bear; at right: Bernard the Bear.

Barnum's Animals Crackers

Who doesn't remember getting a box of Barnum's Animals Crackers as a kid and thinking it was the coolest thing in the world? Nabisco issued six different animals inside boxes that resemble its famous Animals Crackers boxes, with two of them being bears. I ordered my set through the Nabisco website for $44.95: *icat.nabisco.com/nabiscodirect/index.icl* The Brown Bear and Polar Bear retail from $6-$8 each.

Barnum's Animals Crackers Brown Bear and Polar Bear.

Beanie Kids Tutu and Angel.

Beanie Kids

Beanie Kids are Australia's version of Beanie Babies. The set contains many Teddy Bears, many of which are very hard to find. Collector info at *www.beaniekids.com*.

Bear	Price Range
Amber (R)	$7-$8
Angel (R)	$6-$8
Banjo	$6-$8
Berry	$6-$8
Bernard, red ribbon (R)	$16-$20
Bernard, tartan ribbon (R)	$25-$35
Big Billy Blue	$6-$8
Big Purple Penny	$6-$8
Big Red Fred	$6-$8
Blackie	$6-$8
Bluey	$6-$8
Bongo	$6-$8
Chi Chi the panda	$6-$8
Crackle	$6-$8
Fizz	$6-$8
Freeda	$6-$8

Bear	Price Range
Goldilocks	$6-$8
Goldy (R)	$150-$200
Harmony	$6-$8
Herb	$7-$9
Hippy	$6-$8
Jade (R)	$160-$200
Jaffa	$6-$8
Juliet (R)	$6-$8
Kiwi (R)	$8-$10
Kringle	$13-$16
Love, brown, red ribbon (R)	$7-$9
Love, brown, tartan ribbon (R)	$50-$60
Love, tan, red or tartan ribbon (R), each	$50+
Matilda, red ribbon (R)	$50+
Matilda, tartan ribbon (R)	$7-$9
Minty	$6-$8
Nicholas (R)	$6-$8
Noel (R)	$6-$8
Oliver	$6-$8
Ozzie	$8-$10
Polly	$6-$8
Pop	$6-$8
Proud	$6-$8
Romeo (R)	$6-$8
Ruby	$6-$8
Sadie	$6-$8
Smiley (R)	$6-$8
Snap	$6-$8
Sparkle	$6-$8
Spice	$6-$8
Sprinkle	$6-$8
Star	$6-$8
Tingle	$6-$8
TuTu (R)	$6-$8
Twinkle	$6-$8
Violet (R)	$7-$9
Wyatt, Y2K	$7-$9
Y2K	$7-$9
Zap	$6-$8

Bear and Ojo.

Bear in the Big Blue House

Featured on the Disney Channel, "Bear in the Big Blue House" is a great kids' show. Fisher Price had a set of BBBH characters with matching hang tags. Mattel issued the series as part of its Star Beans series with Star Beans tags. The sets' characters are the same, only the tags differ.

Bear	Price Range
Bear	$5-$7
Ojo	$5-$7

Boeing Bears

Aircraft-maker Boeing offers a pair of excellent pilot bears. The 10-inch plush bears have great uniforms and have jointed arms and legs. You can order them through the Boeing gift store at: *active.boeing.com/aboutus/giftshops/flightline/index.cfm?cfid=28288&cftoken=22052.* (By the way, Boeing also offers a really cool astronaut bean bag, as well as one for the Space Shuttle.)

Bear	Price Range
Captain Hale, Commercial Airline Pilot	$15-$18
Major Thorb, Defense Fighter Pilot	$15-$18

From left: Boeing Bears Major Thorb and Captain Hale.

Boyds Bears & Friends

One of the most famous and most popular bear makers of all time is Boyds. This company has produced many wonderful bears over the past 20 years, and there are specific price guides devoted to Boyds.

What's included here are a few recent Boyds Bears lines, just to give you the favor of the quality and style of its bears. These are smaller-sized Boyds that are very affordable and are wonderful to display.

Musical Baby Boyds: Perriwinkle, Buttercup and Honey Snicklefritz.

Baby Boyds Paddy McDoodle.

Blanche de Bearvoire, The Archive Collection.

Bear	Price Range
Baby Boyds	
Buttercup C. Snicklefritz, musical	$6-$8
Dilly McDoodle	$9-$12
Foodle McDoodle	$6-$8
Honey P. Snicklefritz, musical	$6-$8
Paddy McDoodle	$6-$8
Perriwinkle P. Snicklefritz, musical	$6-$8
Boyds (5- to 6-inch)	
Alouetta de Grizetta, cloche hat	$7-$9
Andrei Berriman, in stocking	$9-$12
Andrew Huntington, red jumper	$7-$9
Archibald McBearlie, sweater	$9-$12
Baldwin Bearchild	$7-$9
Becky, red plaid jumper	$7-$9
Becky, green plaid jumper	$7-$9
Bethany Thistlebeary, blue and white dress	$9-$12
Betsey, red plaid dress	$7-$9
Blanche de Bearvoire, green hat	$7-$9
Blackstone, leather collar	$7-$9
Bonnie, denim dress	$9-$12

Echo Goodnight, The Archive Collection.

Bear	Price Range
Boris Berriman, blue and white ski hat	$9-$12
Caledonia, leather collar	$7-$9
Camille de Bear, black felt hat	$9-$12
Cassie Goodnight, angel bear	$7-$9
Chauncey Fitzbruin, sailor hat and collar	$9-$12
Clementine, blue plaid jumper	$7-$9
Colleen O'Bruin, red cape and hood	$7-$9
Echo Goodnight, angel bear	$7-$9
Henley Fitzhampton, blue sailor outfit	$9-$12
Humboldt, leather collar	$7-$9
Jameson J. Bearsford, bow tie	$7-$9
Kinsey Snoopstein, in bunny suit	$7-$9
Lou Bearig, baseball uniform	$7-$9
Laurel S. Berrijam, floral overalls	$7-$9
McKenzie, leather collar	$7-$9
Maya Berriman, sweater and hat	$9-$12
Mindy WiteBruin, blue dress and hat	$15-$20
Minnie Higgenthorpe, straw hat	$9-$12
Natasha Berriman, blue cape and hood	$7-$9
Nikki II, Santa suit	$9-$12
Nod II, polar bear	$7-$9
Serena Goodnight, angel bear	$7-$9
Samuel, red plaid jumper	$7-$9
Sheldon Bearchild, holds red plaid heart	$7-$9
Twila Higgenthorpe, purple felt hat	$9-$12
Yolanda, panda	$7-$9
Yvette Dubeary, black felt hat	$7-$9

Yolanda, The Archive Collection.

Jameson J. Bearsford, The Archive Collection.

Natasha Berriman.

Elfwood and Eastwick Bearington, Mini-Mohair.

Wilbur and Orville, Mini-Mohair.

T.F. Wuzzies (3 inch)
Talbot F. Wuzzie..$5-$7
Tammy F. Wuzzie..$5-$7
Tassel F. Wuzzie ....$5-$7
Tatum F. Wuzzie ....$5-$7
Tilly F. Wuzzie..$5-$7
Timothy F. Wuzzie..$5-$7
Tippy F. Wuzzie..$5-$7
Trevor F. Wuzzie ....$5-$7
Twizzle F. Wuzzie ....$5-$7
Twas F. Wuzzie..$5-$7
Tyler F. Wuzzie..$5-$7
Tyrone F. Wuzzie ....$5-$7

T.F. Wuzzies (5 inch)
T. Farley Wuzzie..$8-$9
T. Frasier Wuzzie ....$8-$9
T. Fulton Wuzzie..$8-$9

Mini-Mohair (4-1/2 inch)
Eastwick Bearington.....................................$9-$12
Elfwood Bearington ....$9-$12
Orville Bearington...$9-$12
Wilbur Bearington ....$9-$12

Twas F. and Tassel F. Wuzzie, T.F. Wuzzies.

Celebrity Bears

Celebrity Bears, issued by JC Bears, are cool. Each has celebrity characteristics providing hints as to whom the bear is modeled. These bears are really catching on among collectors, especially popular superstar versions. The company's website is: *www.celebritybears.com.*

Celebrity Bears–front: Arnold Schwarzenegger, Rosie O'Donnell, Garth Brooks; back: Will Smith, Mel Gibson, Elvis.

Bear	Price Range
#1. Arnold Schwarzenegger (R)	$6-$8
#2. Rosie O'Donnell	$9-$12
#3. Garth Brooks (R)	$8-$12
#4. Will Smith (R)	$6-$8
#5. Mel Gibson (R)	$6-$8
#6. Elvis	$10-$12
#7. Hulk Hogan (R)	$6-$8
#8. Ginger Spice	$6-$8
#9. Michael Jordan (R)	$12-$15
#10. Mariah Carey (R)	$7-$10

#11. Leonardo DiCaprio (R).....................$6-$8
#12. Tiger Woods (R) ....$8-$11
#13. Stephen King.................................$8-$10
#13. Stephen King, white eyes,
    turquoise ribbon (chase bear) ....$14-$20
#14. Sylvester Stallone (R).....................$6-$8
#15. Dennis Rodman (R) ....$6-$8
#16. Shania Twain (R) ....$7-$9
#17. Hanson (R) ....$6-$8
#18. Kate Winslet.................................$9-$12
#19. Indiana Jones (R)...........................$7-$9
#20. Martha Stewart (R) ....$8-$10
#21. Tim Allen (R)................................$6-$8
#22. Whoopi Goldberg (R) ....$8-$10
#23. George Clooney (R)........................$7-$9
#24. Jeff Gordon ....$12-$16
#25. Mark McGwire ....$10-$12
#26. Cher ....$8-$10
#27. Tom Hanks...................................$7-$9
#27. Tom Hanks, *D Day* on vest (chase bear).........$10-$12
#28. Dixie Chicks (R) ....$10-$12
#28. Dixie Chicks, dark blue (chase bear) (R).........$12-$15
#29. Jack Nicholson ....$8-$10
#29. Jack Nicholson, bright yellow (chase bear)........$10-12
#30. Star Wars ....$8-$10
#30. Star Wars, "May the force..." (chase bear) ....$12-$15
#31. John Travolta................................$7-$9
#31. John Travolta, silver metallic thread
    around ball (chase bear) ....$10-$12
#32. Austin Powers ....$7-$9
#32. Austin Powers, blue (chase bear) ....$10-$12
#33. Beatles Bear ....$10-$12
#33. Beatles Bear, "FAB4" (chase bear).....................$12-$14
#34. John Glenn ....$7-$9
#34. John Glenn, "USA" on arm (chase bear)............$8-$10
#35. Goldie Hawn ....$7-$9
#35. Goldie Hawn, background purple (chase bear)...$8-$10
#36. Ricky Martin ....$8-$10
#36. Ricky Martin, Loco for Ricky (chase bear)........$12-$14

Celebrity Bears–front: Hulk Hogan, Ginger Spice, Michael Jordan; back: Mariah Carey, Leonardo DiCaprio, Tiger Woods.

#37. Jimmy Buffet.................................$12-$14
#37. Jimmy Buffet, Margarita on leg,
    blue ribbon (chase bear) ....$16-$20
#38. Julia Roberts.................................$7-$9
#38. Julia Roberts, purple (chase bear) ....$8-$10
#39. Sammy Sosa ....$8-$10
#39. Sammy Sosa, "peace" gesture on arm
    (chase bear) ....$12-$14
#40. John Elway ....$8-$10
#40. John Elway, helmet on arm (chase bear) ....$10-$12
#41. Tin Man ....$7-$9
#42. Scarecrow ....$7-$9
#43. Dorothy ....$7-$9
#44. Cowardly Lion ....$7-$9
#45. Wicked Witch ....$7-$9
#46. Bette Midler ....$8-$10
#47. Adam Sandler ....$7-$9
#48. Darryl Hannah...............................$7-$9
#50. James Stewart................................$7-$9
#51. Jim Carey ....$7-$9
#52. Jeff Daniels..................................$7-$9
#53. Della Reese ....$7-$9
#54. Roma Downey ....$7-$9
#55. Pokeybear....................................$8-$10
Teach, The Golden Rule Bear ....$9-$12
Star 2000 Millennium Bear.......................$8-$12

Cherished Teddies

A new line of bears from Enesco, the Cherished Teddies bean bags are cute and collectible. Be sure to check out Enesco's website at *www.enesco.com*.

Bear	**Price Range**
Ava, bright pink bow	$9-$12
Jackie, light green and white bow	$6-$8
Karen, peach and white bow	$6-$7
Sara, light purple bow	$6-$7
Bear, red heart	$10-$13
Bear, any with T-shirt and sayings, each	$6-$7

Cherished Teddies–top: Hug Me, Miss You, Love Me; bottom: Smile, Best Friends, Need You.

ChillyBears

ChillyBears are bean bag Teddy Bears with a different look than other bears out today. They sit upright, so they're great to display. They are limited to 10,000 of each, and they are hand numbered. The company's website is: *www.chillybears.com.*

Bear	Price Range
Baxter, blue and white stripes	$9-$12
Chilly, brown	$9-$12
Chubby, orange with purple spots	$9-$12
Mae, white with roses	$9-$12
Violet, violet with red balloons	$9-$12

ChillyBears Violet.

ChillyBears Baxter.

Above: ChillyBears Mae; at right: ChillyBears Chubby.

Classic Collecticritters Bear Series I.

Classic Collecticritters

This "celebrity" bear bean bag maker limits its bears to 10,000. Its website is: *www.collecticritters.com*.

Bear	Price Range
Classic Bear Series I	
The Dukester	$10-$15
Frankie	$8-$10
The King	$15-$20
Lucy	$25-$32
Marilyn	$18-$22
Promo Bear Series 1	
Georgia	$30-$40
Homer	$30-$40
Classic Bear Series II	
Bryant	$7-$9
Elton (8,000 made)	$10-$14
Harmony (2,000 made)	$20-$25
Love	$10-$14
Rocky	$7-$9
Shirley	$10-$14
Promo Bears Series II	
Hawaii	$20-$25
T.D.	$20-$25
Jewel Series	
Amber	$10-$14
Emerald	$9-$12
Ruby	$10-$14
Topaz	$9-$12
Turquoise	$10-$14
Red, White and Blue Series	
Blue Senator	$8-$10
Red Senator	$8-$10
White Senator	$8-$10
Ronald McDonald Series	
White, McDonald Charities of So. Cal.	$9-$12
White, Camp McDonald for Good Times	$9-$12
Blue Bear, Loma Linda McDonald House	$9-$12
Red Bear, L.A. McDonald House for Good Times	$9-$12
Yellow Bear, Orange Co. McDonald House	$9-$12

Bear	Price Range
Signature Series	
Buzz Aldrin, silver	$10-$13
Buzz Aldrin, gold, autographed (LE 1,000)	$80-$100
Joe Montana, any color/number, autographed and limited to 1,000, each	$80-$100
Joe Montana #3, green or white jersey	$10-$13
Joe Montana #16, red or white jersey	$10-$13
Joe Montana #19, red jersey	$10-$13
Joe Montana, promo, red/gold jersey (1,000)	$35-$45
Tony Gwynn, purple mini bear, #19	$8-$10
Tony Gwynn, brown bear with uniform #19	$16-$20
Surprise Bear	
Dunk, promo	$18-$22
Texas, promo	$10-$15
VIP Series	
Jackie, VIP I, blue	$26-$32
Jackie, VIP II, burgundy	$18-$22
The Senator, VIP I, gray	$30-$35
The Senator, VIP II, white	$18-$22
The Commander, VIP I, gray	$12-$16
The Commander, VIP II, white	$12-$16
Y2K Millennium Series	
Y, White Bear	$20-$25
2, Gray Bear	$20-$25
K, Black Bear	$20-$25
General	
Amelia Earhart	$7-$10
Cal Ripkin Jr.	$9-$12
Dollie	$10-$12
Dunk (promo)	$12-$14
Elizabeth	$10-$12
Euro Bear	$10-$12
Garfield	$16-$24
I Love Lucy	$22-$30
James Dean	$16-$20
Marilyn Monroe	$16-$22

Classy Tassy's: Peaches Gorja and Rip Van Twinkle.

Classy Tassy's Bears

Classy Tassy's Bears represent states and are super quality. Weighing about a half-pound each, these are some of the heaviest bean bags around. The company said it intends to produce a bean bag bear for each state, plus the District of Columbia. One green-and-white pajama Rip Van Twinkle was produced for every 11 red-and-white pajama versions. Maureena Marina will have her flags changed from time to time. The company's website is: *www.classytassy.com*.

Bear	Price Range
Abbey Applelet (New York)	$7-$10
Blu Jean (Louisiana)	$7-$10
Dallas Starr (Texas)	$7-$10
Felicia Flamingo (Florida)	$7-$10
J.R. Casino (USA)	$7-$10
Kiddie Jubilee (Birthday), blue or pink	$7-$10
Maureena Marina (New Jersey)	$7-$10
Ms. Society (California)	$7-$10
Oops Bartholomeu, green (North Carolina)	$7-$10
Oops Bartholomeu, orange (North Carolina)	$7-$10

Bear	Price Range
Oops Bartholomeu, pink (North Carolina)	$7-$10
Orchid Maui (Hawaii)	$7-$10
Peaches Gorja (Georgia)	$7-$10
Riblet Montgomery (Ohio)	$7-$10
Rip Van Twinkle, red/white pajamas (Wyoming)	$7-$10
Rip Van Twinkle, green/white pajamas (Wyoming)	$8-$12
Terri Tanasi (Tennessee)	$7-$10
Wolfy Wolverine (Michigan)	$7-$10

#105, #104, #106.

Above: #171, #169, #167; right: (top) #109 and (bottom) #110, #112, #111.

Coca-Cola Bean Bag Plush

Cola bean bag plush sets are very popular among bean bag collectors and Coca-Cola collectors. The famous polar bear is featured in nearly every set. Several exclusive Coke bean bags are starting to draw big dollars. The Coca-Cola Bean Bag Plush are made by Cavanagh. Check out Cavanagh's website at *www.cavanaghgrp.com*.

Bear	Price Range
Spring 1997 (R)	
Polar Bear, baseball cap, #111	$18-$22
Polar Bear, pink bow, #110	$18-$22
Polar Bear, T-shirt, #112	$18-$22
Polar Bear, holding bottle, #109	$18-$22
Holiday 1997 (R)	
Polar Bear, plaid bow, #105	$10-$12
Polar Bear, red bow, #106	$10-$12

Bear	Price Range
Polar Bear, snowflake cap, #104	$10-$12
Heritage I, 1998 (R)	
Polar Bear, driver's cap, #140	$9-$11
Polar Bear, sweater, #116	$9-$11
Heritage II, 1998 (R)	
Polar Bear, cap and scarf, #167	$8-$10
Polar Bear, blue ski cap, #169	$8-$10
Polar Bear, soda fountain clothes, #171	$8-$10

#131.

#120 and
#118.

#151 and #126.

#184.

Bear	Price Range
Everyday, 1998 (R)	
Polar Bear, argyle shirt, #131	$7-$9
Winter, 1998 (R)	
Polar Bear, red scarf, #120	$7-$9
Polar Bear, snowflake hat, #118	$7-$9
Sport, 1999	
Polar Bear, baseball, #261	$6-$8
Polar Bear, skiing, #265	$6-$8
Polar Bear, golf, #264	$6-$8
Polar Bear, football, #262	$6-$8
Everyday, 1999	
Polar Bear, shirt, #200	$6-$8
Polar Bear, baseball cap, #199	$6-$8
Polar Bear, scarf, #201	$6-$8
Winter, 1999	
Polar Bear, snowflake hat and vest, #208	$6-$8
Polar Bear, striped hat and scarf, #206	$6-$8
Polar Bear, striped shirt and scarf, #209	$6-$8
Blockbuster Exclusives, 1997 (R)	
Polar Bear, driver's cap, #146	$10-$15
Polar Bear, green bow, #144	$10-$15
Polar Bear, vest, #149	$10-$15
Coca-Cola Collector's Society	
Polar Bear, sweater, LE 1998, #151 (R)	$20-$25
Polar Bear, polka-dot collar, LE 1999, #126	$13-$16
Coca-Cola Store Exclusives	
Polar Bear, Collector Classic T-shirt, #184	$15-$18
Polar Bear, city on shirt (Atlanta or Las Vegas), #191	$13-$16
Polar Bear, red scarf, #159	$16-$20

#161 and #163.

#153 and #154.

Gift Creation Concept Retailer Exclusive
Polar Bear, hat and vest, #166 ....$13-$16
Polar Bear, red romper, #267 ....$16-$20

Manchu Wok Restaurants Exclusive
Bear, Chinese shirt, #177....................................$10-$12

Media Play Exclusives, 1998
Polar Bear, shirt, #161 ....$12-$16
Polar Bear, holiday scarf, #163..........................$12-$16

Musicland Exclusive (R)
Polar Bear, snowflake cap, #113........................$25-$30

Parade of Gifts Exclusive
Polar Bear, trademark vest, #165 ....$8-$10

White's Kissing Bears (R)
Polar Bear, green bow, #153 (LE 15,000) ....$18-$22
Polar Bear, jumper (LE 15,000) ....$10-$12

Polar Bear, red/white scarf, #154 (LE 15,000)....$18-$22
Polar Bear, red bow (LE 15,000)........................$10-$12

World of Coca-Cola Exclusives
Polar Bear, black tux, red tie, #193 ....$12-$16
Polar Bear, red bow tie, red bow, #194..............$12-$16
Polar Bear, gray hooded sweatshirt, #269 ....$12-$16
Polar Bear, serving jacket and hat, #274 ....$12-$16

Australia Exclusive, 1998 (Hungry Jacks)
Polar Bear, female, bow.....................................$16-$20
Polar Bear, male, scarf ....$16-$20

1999 Coca-Cola International Bean Bag Collection
7. Quala the Koala Bear, Australia, #220 ....$7-$8
18. Zongshi the Panda Bear, China, #228 ....$7-$8
25. Barris the Brown Bear, Russia, #235...............$7-$8
25. Baris the Brown Bear (Canada issue), Russia, #235 ....$7-$9

CoCo Wheats Bear

This advertising bean bag bear was a promotion through CoCo Wheats.

Bear	**Price Range**
CoCo Wheats Bear	$8-$10

CoCo Wheats bean bag bear.

Colgate-Palmolive Starlight Bears.

Creative Memories Scrappie.

Colgate-Palmolive Starlight Bears

Excellent set of bean bag bears was issued in certain parts of the country in 1998. They were available with the purchase of Colgate-Palmolive products. Made by A&A Plush.

Bear	Price Range
Brown	.$6-$8
Green	.$6-$8
Midnight blue	.$6-$8
White	.$6-$8

Creative Memories "Scrappie" the Bear

Creative Memories, a leading maker of scrapbooks and supplies, issued a cute bean bag bear named "Scrappie" as an incentive to Creative Memories' consultants only upon placing a qualifying order. The promotion must have worked well because a second offering of another great bear, "Rita," was offered in the fall of 1999. Both bears will be difficult for collectors to find.

Bear	Price Range
Rita (white)	.$8-$10
Scrappie (brown)	.$50-$65

Disney Brer Bear (Song of the South).

Disney Baloo Bear (Jungle Book).

Disney Mini Bean Bag Plush Bears

The 1967 film Jungle Book and the 1946 film Song of the South featured a couple of memorable bears. (Also see "Winnie the Pooh" section.)

Bear	Price Range
The Jungle Book	
Baloo	$8-$10
Song of the South	
Brer Bear	$8-$10

Ganz Wee Bear Village

Ganz, a long-time, high-quality bear maker has come out with a winning set called "Wee Bear Village," featuring some of the smallest and cutest bears around. These tiny 5-inch plush bears are disguised in a variety of animal and other outfits. Since they're small and jointed, collectors can neatly display several in a small area. They're also not expensive on the retail level ($6-$7 each). You can find these bears and other Ganz bears at finer gift shops. Ganz has a website at *www.ganz.com*.

Bear	Price Range
Buggables Series	
Bumble Bumblebee	$7-$10
Butterfly	$7-$10
Lucky Ladybug	$7-$10
Willow Bug	$7-$10
Christmas Series	
Chilly Snowman	$7-$10
Ginger Gingerbread Man	$7-$10
Kringle Santa	$6-$8
Rudy Reindeer	$6-$8
Squeeks Mouse	$12-$16
Tux Penguin	$12-$16
Dinosaur Series	
Fossil	$8-$12
Sara	$6-$8
Spike	$6-$8
T-Rex	$8-$12

Bear	Price Range
Tops	$8-$12
Easter Series	
Curly Lamb	$7-$10
Hops Bunny	$6-$8
Quacks Duck	$6-$8
Farm Series	
Clover Cow	$6-$8
Doodle Rooster	$6-$7
Frisky Cat	$6-$7
Leap Frog	$6-$7
Mudford Pig	$6-$7
Paws Dog	$6-$7
Flower Series	
Li'l Blossom Pansy	$7-$10
Li'l Blossom Rose	$10-$14
Li'l Blossom Sunflower	$7-$10
Halloween Series	
Devil	$6-$8
Esmerelda Witch	$6-$8
Mr. Bones Skeleton	$6-$8
Pumpkinhead Pumpkin	$6-$8
Jungle Series	
Congo Monkey	$6-$7
Jumbo Elephant	$8-$12
King Lion	$6-$7
Saber Tiger	$6-$8
Stretch Giraffe	$7-$10
Stripes Zebra	$6-$8

Ginger Gingerbread Man.

Garfield's Pooky

Garfield the cat has his favorite little bear named Pooky. Available in the "Garfield Stuff" catalog (888-374-PAWS) or online at: *www.catalog.garfield.com*.

Bear	Price Range
Pooky	$8-$10

Garfield's Pooky Bear.

Girl Scouts Bears

"Belly Beans" is the name of Girl Scout bean bags from Mary Meyer. Each of the first sets has a bear.

Brownie Girl Scout Bear.

Bear	Price Range
Belly Beans Set #1	
Brownie Girl Scout Bear	$9-$12
Belly Beans Set #2	
American Panda	$13-$16

Godiva Bear

Godiva is my favorite chocolate, so I was very happy to see the company offer an exclusive bean bag bear with the purchase of its chocolate. With its holiday 1999 offering, the bear is just not plush, but mighty cute! As you can well imagine, I'm hoping the bear with chocolate promotions are continued in the future! I ordered these bears through the Godiva catalogs during 1999.

Bear	Price Range
1999 Godiva Valentine Bear (R)	$14-$18
1999 Holiday Bear	$12-$15

Godiva Valentine Bear.

Front row: Stagger Lee, Sugaree, Althea; back row: Samson, Tennessee Jed.

Front row: Jack Straw, Cosmic Charlie, St. Stephen; back row: Bertha, Cassidy.

Grateful Dead Bears

The Bean Bears: Simply put, Grateful Dead Bean Bears are some of the hottest bears on the market. The key is that these bears are so colorful, cute and unique that people other than Dead Heads are collecting them. Look for the Delilah bear *without* the black pads on her hands. I was told by the bean bears' maker, Liquid Blue, that just 11,000 of this variation/error were made.

The Plush Bears: Liquid Blue's Grateful Dead Plush Bears stand 10 to 12 inches high and are available in a variety of striking colors. They are a perfect complement to the Grateful Dead Bean Bears. The plush bears are no longer in production, so I expect a rise in value for these bears in the next year or two.

Grateful Dead Bean Bears

Bear	Price Range
Set I (1997)	
Althea (R), Qty. 49,920	$15-$18
Bertha (R) Qty. 84,096	$9-$12
Cassidy (R), Qty. 85,824	$8-$10
Cosmic Charlie (R), Qty. 134,592	$8-$10
Delilah, black pads on hands (R), Qty. 55,464	$20-$25
Delilah, w/o black hand pads (R), Qty. 11,000	$50-$60
Jack Straw (R), Qty. 49,920	$14-$18
St. Stephen (R), Qty. 108,576	$8-$10
Samson (R), Qty. 90,048	$8-$10

From left: Delilah with black paws (common), Delilah without black paws (rare).

Stagger Lee (R), Qty. 86,688 ....$8-$10
Sugaree (R), Qty. 57,600 ....$25-$30
Tennessee Jed (R), Qty. 56,256 ....$16-$20

Set II (1998)
Crazy Fingers ....$8-$10
Dark Star (R), Qty. 131,040 ....$8-$10
Daydream (R), Qty. 101,376 ....$8-$10
Dupree (R), Qty. 106,080................................$8-$10
Franklin (R) Qty. 106,464 ....$8-$10
Irie (R), Qty. 97,824 ....$9-$12
Jerry...$8-$10
Peggy-O (R), Qty. 117,984 ....$8-$10
Ripple (R), Qty. 108,864 ....$8-$10
Sunshine (R), Qty. 104,064...............................$8-$10

Set III
Ashbury...$8-$10
August West ....$8-$10
Blues Man ....$8-$10
China Cat ....$8-$10
Daisy...$8-$10
Doodah Man ....$8-$10
Esau ....$8-$10
Foolish Heart ....$8-$10
Haight ....$8-$10
Pearly Baker ....$8-$10
Reuben ....$8-$10
Uncle Sam...$8-$10

Set IV
Candy Man ....$8-$10
Deal ....$8-$10
Fall Tour ....$8-$10
Father Time ....$8-$10
Fire ....$8-$10
Jack A Roe ....$8-$10
Lost Sailor ....$8-$10
Scarlet...$8-$10
Snow Flake ....$8-$10
Terrapin (turtle) ....$8-$10
Uncle John ....$8-$10

Limited Edition
All Access, LE ....$35-$38
Black Peter, LE 30,000 (R) ....$35-$45
Casey Jones, LE...$38-$45
Touch of Grey, LE..$38-$45

Front row: Dark Star, Peggy-O, Crazy Fingers; back row: Daydream, Sunshine.

Front row: Ripple, Dupree, Irie; back row: Franklin, Jerry.

Grateful Teddy Bears

Bear	Price Range
Blue (R)	$12-$15
Brown, goggles, white scarf (Pilot) (R)	$12-$15
Fuscia (R)	$12-$15
Green (R)	$12-$15
Green (Alien) (R)	$15-$20
Lime green (R)	$12-$15
"Miracle," brown	$12-$15
Purple (R)	$12-$15
Red (R)	$12-$15
"Sage," green	$12-$15
"Spirit," purple	$12-$15
"Stella Blue," blue	$12-$15
Tan, green hat, dreadlocks (Rasta)	$12-$15
Teal (R)	$12-$15
White with black polka-dots (R)	$12-$15
Yellow (R)	$12-$15

Limited Edition Black Peter.

Hot Shots bean bag bears.

Gund

Gund bean bags are well made. The Hot Shots bean bag bears are pretty cute and colorful. You will find Gund bean bags in better quality gift stores.

Bear	Price Range
Hot Shots Bears: any of 10 colors, each	$6-$8
Slider the bear	$6-$8
Snuffy the bear, chocolate brown	$6-$8
Snuffy the bear, tan brown	$6-$8
Tender Teddy the bear, dark brown	$6-$8

Harley-Davidson Bean Bag Plush

The Harley-Davidson Bean Bag Plush characters, about half of which are bears, were first released in 1997. With their stylish biker costumes, they are popular in the Harley and bean bag collecting communities. Made by Cavanagh: *www.cavanaghgrp.com.*

Bear	Price Range
Set 1 (1997) (R)	
Big Twin bear	$8-$10
Motorhead bear	$8-$10
Roamer bear	$8-$10
Set 2 (1998)	
Evo bear	$7-$9
Kickstart bear	$7-$9
Manifold Max bear	$7-$9
Set 3 (1999)	
Bravo bear	$8-$10
Limited Edition	
Tank the bear	$25-$30

Harley-Davidson Tank.

Harley-Davidson Big Twin, Motorhead, Roamer.

Harley-Davidson Evo, Kickstart, Manifold Max.

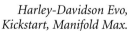

Limited Treasures Elvis, Gordon, Sam, Sherlock; at right is Elvis in his Treasure Box.

Limited Treasures

These bean bag bears depicting celebrities, holiday themes and sports stars. Nice quality, and those packed in their own "treasure boxes" are very nice. The "test" and "chase" bears are the most collectible of the lot. Limited Treasures has a website at: *www.limitedtreasures.com*.

Bear	Price Range

1st Issue (R)

Elvis, blue	$25-$30
Elvis, test bear	$40-$50
Elvis, white chase bear	$55-$70
Gordon	$20-$25
Gordon, test bear	$40-$50
Sam	$11-$13
Sam, test bear	$26-$32
Sherlock	$11-$13
Sherlock, test bear	$18-$22

2nd Issue, Holiday Collection (R)

Bear Claus	$4-$5
Celebration, blue chase bear	$18-$22
Celebration, gold chase bear	$60-$75
Celebration, green chase bear	$18-$22
Celebration, purple chase bear	$18-$22

3rd Issue, NFL Bears

Premium Pro Bears Series I (R)

Barry Sanders #20	$5-$7
Barry Sanders #20, white chase bear	$18-$22
Brett Favre #4	$5-$7
Brett Favre #4, test	$12-$15
Brett Favre #4, white chase bear	$20-$25
Charles Woodson #24	$5-$7
Charles Woodson #24, white chase bear	$12-$15
Dan Marino #13	$5-$7
Dan Marino #13, white chase bear	$18-$22
Deion Sanders #21	$5-$7
Deion Sanders #21, white chase bear	$12-$16
Doug Flutie #7	$5-$7
Doug Flutie #7, white chase bear	$12-$16
Drew Bledsoe #11	$5-$7
Drew Bledsoe #11, white chase bear	$14-$18
Jerry Rice #80	$5-$7
Jerry Rice #80, white chase bear	$14-$18
Mark Brunell #8	$5-$7
Mark Brunell #8, white chase bear	$12-$16
Peyton Manning #18	$5-$7
Peyton Manning #18, white chase bear	$12-$16
Randy Moss #84	$5-$7
Randy Moss #84, test	$12-$15
Randy Moss #84, white chase bear	$20-$25

Premier Edition

LT Pro Premium Bears II: John Elway.

LT Pro Premium Bears I, chase: Dan Marino (front view).

Terrell Davis #30	$5-$7
Terrell Davis #30, white chase bear	$14-$18

Premium Pro Bears Series II (R)

Charlie Batch #10	$5-$7
Charlie Batch #10, white chase bear	$12-$15
Eddie George #27	$5-$7
Eddie George #27, white chase bear	$12-$15
Emmitt Smith #22	$5-$7
Emmitt Smith #22, white chase bear	$14-$18
Jake Plummer #16	$5-$7
Jake Plummer #16, white chase bear	$12-$16
John Elway #7, blue	$5-$7
John Elway #7, orange	$8-$10
John Elway #7, test	$10-$12
John Elway #7, white chase bear	$18-$22
Jamal Anderson #32	$5-$7
Jamal Anderson #32, white chase bear	$12-$16
Keyshawn Johnson #19	$5-$7
Keyshawn Johnson #19, white chase bear	$12-$16
Randall Cunningham #17	$5-$7
Randall Cunningham #17, white chase bear	$12-$16
Ryan Leaf #16	$5-$7
Ryan Leaf #16, white chase bear	$10-$12
Steve Young #8	$5-$7
Steve Young #8, test	$10-$12

LT Pro Premium Bears I: Terrell Davis.

Above: LT Pro Premium Bears I: Randy Moss; left: LT Pro Premium Bears I, chase: Randy Moss.

Steve Young #8, white chase bear ....$12-$16
Troy Aikman #8 ....$5-$7
Troy Aikman #8, white chase bear.....................$14-$18
Vinny Testaverde #16 ....$5-$7
Vinny Testaverde #16, white chase bear ....$12-$15

Premium Pro Bears Series III (R)
Carl Pickens #81 ....$5-$7
Chris Carter #80 ....$5-$7
Chris Chandler #12 ....$5-$7
Curtis Martin #28..$5-$7
Ed McCaffrey #87 ....$5-$7
Fred Taylor #28 ....$5-$7
Garrison Hearst #20 ....$5-$7
Jerome Bettis #36..$5-$7
Joey Galloway #84 ....$5-$7
John Randle #93 ....$5-$7
Junior Seau #55 ....$5-$7
Kordell Stewart #10..$5-$7
Marshall Faulk #28 ....$5-$7
Mike Alstott #40 ....$5-$7
Reggie White #92..$5-$7
Rich Gannon, #12..$5-$7
Robert Edwards #47 ....$5-$7
Shannon Sharpe #84 ....$5-$7

Steve Beuerlein #7 ....$5-$7
Steve McNair #9 ....$5-$7
Terrell Owens #81 ....$5-$7
Terry Glenn #88...$5-$7
Tony Boselli #71 ....$5-$7
Warrick Dunn #28..$5-$7
Wayne Chrebet #80 ....$5-$7
Zach Thomas #54 ....$5-$7

Denver Broncos Super Bowl Champions (tie-dye)
Terrell Davis...$7-$9
John Elway (blue tie-dye) ....$7-$9
John Elway (white, MVP) ....$8-$10
Ed McCaffrey...$5-$6
Bill Romanoski ....$5-$6
Shannon Sharpe ....$5-$6

Super Bowl Bear
Super Bowl NFL Players Bear...........................$18-$22

L.A. Dodgers Beanpals

Beanpal's produced this sharp-looking bear, sold by the Los Angeles Dodgers baseball team in 1997.

Bear	**Price Range**
Bearbino Bear (R)	$12-$16

Mall of American Teddy Bears.

Mall of America Bears

Set of four of excellent Teddy Bear bean bags with "Mall of America" embroidered on them. Sold as souvenirs at Minnesota's Mall of America.

Bear	Price Range
Blue Teddy Bear	$9-$12
Brown Teddy Bear	$9-$12
Cream Teddy Bear	$9-$12
Red Teddy Bear	$9-$12

Meanies

Their name says it all. The Meanies have grown in popularity and collectibility throughout 1998 and 1999. The company's website is www.meanies.com.

Bear	Price Range
Series 2	
Bare Bear, red mouth	$5-$6
Bare Bear, pink mouth	$5-$6
Burny the Bear	$8-$10
Series 3	
Tied the Bear, white rope	$8-$10
Tied the Bear, black rope (LE 10,000)	$25-$30
Valentine's 1999	
Heartless Bear, red (LE 7,500)	$25-$30
Heartless Bear, white	$6-$8

Bare Bear and Burny the Bear.

White Heartless Bear and red Heartless Bear.

OshKosh B'gosh bean bag bear (shoot).

Paddington Bear

The children's character, Paddington Bear, was made into two bean bags in 1998. Produced by Kid's Gifts, I found my set at a Sears store.

Bear	Price Range
Paddington, red coat	$6-$7
Paddington, yellow coat	$6-$7

From left (bottom) Hugs, Kisses; (middle) Grizwald, Patty; (top): Crystal, Violet, Benny.

OshKosh B'gosh Bean Bag Bear

Very cute and well-made bean bag bear from one of my favorite clothing makers-OshKosh B'gosh. I found this bear at an OshKosh B'gosh outlet store in 1999 for $5.99. Doesn't he look a little like Winnie the Pooh?

Bear	Price Range
OshKosh B'gosh bean bag bear	$7-$10

Paddington Bear bean bags.

Puffkins

One of the best things about Puffkins bears is they are great for displaying, as they are the same size and shape. These little bundles of joy have a legion of diehard collectors. At this time, none of the bears are pricey, so they are easy to locate. Puffkins has a great website offering lots of collector information at *www.swibco.com*.

Bear	Price Range
Aussie the koala	$5-$7
Benny the bear	$5-$7
Buttercup the bear	$5-$7
Cosmo the bear	$5-$7
Crystal the bear	$5-$7
Grizwald the bear	$5-$7
Honey the bear (R)	$6-$8
Hugs the bear	$5-$7
Jingles the bear (R)	$7-$9

Bear	Price Range
Kisses the bear	$5-$7
Mango the bear	$5-$7
Patrick the bear	$5-$7
Patty the bear	$5-$7

Bear	Price Range
Peter the panda	$5-$7
Rosie the bear	$6-$8
Skylar the bear	$5-$7
Telly the bear	$5-$7
Violet the bear	$5-$7

Salvino's Bammers

Salvino's Bammers is a great line of officially licensed, limited-edition bears. They are the only bean bag products allowed to use the names and numbers of Major League Baseball players! Because of Bammers' popularity, Salvino has branched out into other sports and entertainment. For more information, go to: *www.bammers.com*.

Promo Bammers

Bear (with COA)	Price Range
Muhammad Ali (tie-dyed)	$14-$20
Kobe Bryant (yellow/purple lettering)	$12-$18
John Elway (orange/blue lettering)	$18-$24
Wayne Gretzky (full-size, blue lettering)	$10-$15
Tara Lipinski (light blue)	$35-$45
Mark McGwire (red)	$110-$125
Sammy Sosa (blue tie-dye)	$18-22

Family Series (Hallmark Store exclusives)

Mark McGwire (large, mid-sized, small) ....$12-$16

Baseball Bammers

1998 Commemorative Gold Set (R)

Bear	Price Range
Dante Bichette (purple)	$25-$30
Juan Gonzalez (red)	$15-$20
Ken Griffey Jr. (green)	$15-$20
Tony Gwynn (creamy gold)	$40-$45
Derek Jeter (white)	$12-$20
Greg Maddux (gray)	$12-$20
Mark McGwire (red)	$30-$40
Mike Piazza (white)	$15-$25
Cal Ripken Jr (orange)	$20-$30
Gary Sheffield (blue)	$12-$20
Frank Thomas (white)	$12-$20
Kerry Wood (blue)	$12-$20

1998 Rocky's All Star Set (Colorado) (R)

Bear	Price Range
Dante Bichette (purple)	$30-$40
Vinny Castilla (purple)	$30-$45
Larry Walker (purple)	$30-$45

Promo Bammers (from left): Mark McGwire, John Elway, Wayne Gretzky and Sammy Sosa.

1998 Summer Edition–top: Cal Ripken Jr., Barry Bonds, Mark McGwire, Alex Rodriguez, Sammy Sosa, Ivan Rodriguez, Chipper Jones; bottom: Jim Edmonds, Ken Griffey Jr., Tino Martinez, Roger Clemens, David Justice.

1998 Summer Edition (R)

Barry Bonds (orange) ....$6-$8	Tino Martinez (gold) ....$6-$8
Roger Clemens (blue) ....$6-$8	Mark McGwire (purple) ....$7-$9
Jim Edmonds (white)..$6-$8	Cal Ripken Jr. (dark blue)....................................$6-$8
Ken Griffey Jr. (tie-dye) ....$6-$8	Alex Rodriguez (tie-dye)......................................$6-$8
Chipper Jones (lavendar)....................................$6-$8	Ivan Rodriguez (cream) ....$6-$8
David Justice (maroon)...$6-$8	Sammy Sosa (red) ....$7-$9

1998 Holiday Set.

1998 Holiday Set (R)

Ken Griffey Jr..$6-$8	Mark McGwire ....$7-$9
Chipper Jones ....$6-$8	Cal Ripken Jr...$6-$8
Dave Justice...$6-$8	Alex Rodriguez ....$6-$8

Bammers 1998 Roberto Clemente.

Bammers 1998 Home Run Kings Set.

Bear	**Price Range**

1998 Roberto Clemente (R)
Roberto Clemente (gold w/Puerto Rico flag)...$15-$20

1998 Home Run Kings Set
Roger Maris ....$6-$7
Mark McGwire ....$7-$9
Babe Ruth ....$6-$8
Sammy Sosa ....$7-$9

1998 New York Yankees World Series Set
Scott Brosius ....$5-$6
Orlando Hernandez ....$5-$6
Derek Jeter ....$5-$7
Tino Martinez..$5-$6
Darryl Strawberry ....$5-$6
David Wells...$5-$6

Bammers 1998 New York Yankees World Series Set.

Bammers 1998 Award Winners Set.

1998 Award Winners Set

Roger Clemens..$4-$6	Ken Griffey Jr. ....$4-$6
Tom Glavine ....$4-$6	Mark McGwire ....$4-$6
Juan Gonzalez...$4-$6	Sammy Sosa ....$4-$6
Ben Grieve ....$4-$6	Kerry Wood..$4-$6

1999 Opening Day Bammers Baseball Set–top: Derek Jeter, Nomar Garciaparra, Sammy Sosa, J.D. Drew; middle: Mo Vaughn, Mark McGwire, Mike Piazza, Jeff Bagwell, Kerry Wood, Randy Johnson; bottom: Roger Clemens, Albert Belle.

Bear	Price Range

1999 Opening Day Baseball
Jeff Bagwell (white/gold stars) ....$5-$7
Albert Belle (orange/black) ....$5-$7
Roger Clemens (black/white) ....$6-$8
J.D. Drew (red/white) ....$6-$8
Nomar Garciaparra (red/blue) ....$6-$8
Derek Jeter (white/black pinstripes) ....$6-$8
Randy Johnson (green/purple) ....$6-$8
Mark McGwire (red/white) ....$7-$9
Mike Piazza (blue/red) ....$6-$8
Sammy Sosa (blue/red, white and blue) ....$7-$9
Mo Vaughn (blue/gold) ....$6-$8
David Wells (black/white) ....$5-$7
Kerry Wood (red/white/blue) ....$5-$7

1999 Fourth of July Set
Ken Griffey Jr. ....$10-$15
Derek Jeter ....$10-$15
Mark McGwire ....$10-$15
Mike Piazza ....$10-$15
Cal Ripken Jr. ....$10-$15
Sammy Sosa ....$10-$15

1999 Baby Bammers (sold as pair on blister pack)
Mark McGwire and J.D. Drew ....$8-$12

Dante Bichette and Larry Walker ....$8-$12
Kevin Brown and Gary Sheffield.....................$8-$12
Tony Gwynn and Wally Joyner ....$8-$12
Jeff Bagwell and Ken Caminiti.........................$8-$12
Sammy Sosa and Mark Grace...........................$8-$12
Mike Piazza and Robin Ventura ....$8-$12
Derek Jeter and Roger Clemens.......................$8-$12
Derek Jeter and David Wells ....$8-$12
Cal Ripken Jr. and Will Clark ....$8-$12
Nomar Garciaparra and John Valentin ....$8-$12
Roberto Alomar and Sandy Alomar................$8-$12
Tim Salmon and Darin Erstad ....$8-$12
Juan Gonzalez and Rusty Greer.......................$8-$12
Wade Boggs and Jose Canseco..........................$8-$12
Ken Griffey Jr. and Edgar Martinez.................$8-$12
Jason Giambi and Ben Grieve..........................$8-$12

1999 Baby Bammers prototypes
Wayne Gretzky (blue/gold lettering).............$15-$20

1999 International Set
Juan Gonzalez (Puerto Rico) ....$6-$8
Chan Ho Park (Korea) ....$5-$7
Andruw Jones (Curacao) ....$5-$7

Bear	Price Range

1999 Red Sox All Star Set (Boston)
Nomar Garciaparra ....$7-$9
Tom Gordon ....$6-$8
Pedro Martinez ....$7-$9

1999 Nolan Ryan Set
Nolan Ryan with California Angels.......................$6-$9
Nolan Ryan with Houston Astros ....$6-$9
Nolan Ryan with New York Mets ....$6-$9
Nolan Ryan with Texas Rangers ....$6-$9

1999 Mark McGwire Home Run Set
Mark McGwire 100 Home Runs ....$8-$12
Mark McGwire 200 Home Runs ....$8-$12
Mark McGwire 300 Home Runs ....$8-$12

Bear	Price Range

Mark McGwire 400 Home Runs ....$8-$12
Mark McGwire 500 Home Runs ....$8-$12

1999 7th Inning Stretch Set
Craig Biggio ....$12-$15
Jose Canseco ....$7-$10
Ken Griffey Jr. ....$9-$12
Tony Gwynn ....$9-$12
Rickey Henderson ....$7-$10
Mark McGwire ....$15-$18
Raul Mondesi ....$7-$10
Cal Ripken Jr..$12-$15
Scott Rolen...$15-$18
Frank Thomas ....$7-$10
Bernie Williams ....$7-$10
Matt Williams...$7-$10

Sports-Event Giveaways

Bear	Price Range
Henry Aaron, LA Dodgers, 4/8/99 (27,000)	$10-$15
Michael Barrett, Harrisburg Senators, 6/18/99	$75-$90
Duke, Albuquerque Dukes, 6/27/99	n/a
Jim Edmonds, California Angels, 5/1/99 (10,000)	$15-$20
Alex Fernandez, Florida Marlins, 5/1/99 (20,000)	$25-$35
Cliff Floyd, Harrisburg Senators	n/a
Ken Griffey Jr., LA Dodgers, 4/11/99 (27,000)	$10-$15
Vladimir Guerrero, Harrisburg Senators, 5/22/99	$40-$60
Derek Jeter, Columbus Clippers, 7/4/99	$15-$20
Bobby "Jonesy" Jones, Tulsa Drillers, 5/2/99	n/a
Paul Kariya, Mighty Ducks, 1/10/99 (3,500)	$40-$50
Roger Maris, LA Dodgers, 4/10/99 (27,000)	$10-$15
Mark McGwire, Columbus Clippers, 4/16/99	n/a
Mark McGwire, LA Dodgers, 4/6/99 (27,000)	$15-$20
Mark McGwire, Reading Phillies, 6/18/99	n/a
Scott Rolen, Philadelphia Phillies, 5/17/99 (17,000)	$18-$24
Scott Rolen, Reading Phillies, 7/11/99	n/a
Babe Ruth, LA Dodgers, 4/7/99 (27,000)	$10-$15
Nolan Ryan, SSPC	n/a
Nolan Ryan, Texas Rangers	n/a
Tim Salmon, California Angels, 9/18/99 (10,000)	n/a
Curt Schilling, Reading Phillies, 7/26/99	n/a
Teemu Selanne, Mighty Ducks, 1/10/99 (3,500)	$40-$50

Bammers Teemu Selanne given away at Mighty Ducks game on 1/10/99.

Bear	Price Range
Sammy Sosa, Columbus Clippers, 4/16/99	$20-$25
Sammy Sosa, LA Dodgers, 4/9/99 (27,000)	$10-$15
Sammy Sosa, Reading Phillies, 8/10/99	n/a
Mo Vaughn, California Angels, 5/15/99 (10,000)	$20-$25
Bernie Williams, Columbus Clippers, 5/31/99	$40-$50

1999 Salvino's Bammers Collector's Club
Mark McGwire, furry (brown/red) ....$25-$35

1999 Team Best Set
Ryan Anderson (Wisconsin Timber Rattlers).........$9-$11
Rick Ankiel (Peoria Chiefs)....................................$10-$12
Lance Berkman (New Orleans Zephyrs)...............$10-$12
Pat Burrell (Clearwater Phillies)........................$20-$24
J.D. Drew (Memphis Redbirds) ....$12-$18
J.D. Drew (Arkansas Travelers) ....$12-$18

1999 Signature Series

Henry Aaron, LE 715..$120-$150

Kareem Abdul-Jabber LE 1,969 ....$70-$90
Joe Montana, LE 1,979 ....$70-$90
Joe Namath, LE 1,969...$80-$100

Homerun Club

Jeff Bagwell...$6-$8
Carlos Delgado ....$6-$8
Ken Griffey Jr. ....$7-$9
Mark McGwire...$8-$10
Alex Rodriguez..$7-$9
Sammy Sosa ....$8-$10

Basketball Bammers

1999 Los Angeles Lakers
Kareem Abdul-Jabber..$5-$7
Kobe Bryant ....$5-$7
Wilt Chamberlain ....$5-$7
Magic Johnson ....$5-$7
Jerry West ....$5-$7

From left: Magic Johnson, Jerry West, Kobe Bryant, Kareem Abdul-Jabber and Wilt Chamberlain.

Football Bammers

Bear	Price Range
1999 Football Series I (R)	
Troy Aikman	$9-$12
Bubby Brister	$9-$12
Chris Chandler	$5-$7
Randall Cunningham	$5-$7
Terrell Davis (blue)	$6-$8
Brett Favre	$7-$10
John Elway (orange)	$7-$10
Doug Flutie	$8-$10
Peyton Manning	$5-$7
Dan Marino	$7-$9

1999 Bammers Terrell Davis orange and blue.

1999 Bammers John Elway blue and orange.

Joe Namath Signature Series Bammer.

1999 Bammers Football set.

Bear	Price Range
Donovan McNabb	$5-$7
Jake Plummer	$5-$7
Barry Sanders	$8-$10
Ricky Williams	$5-$7

1999 Super Bowl Legends Set

Terry Bradshaw	$6-$8
Brett Favre	$6-$8
John Elway	$7-$10
Joe Montana (San Francisco 49ers)	$7-$10
Joe Namath (New York Jets)	$6-$8
Steve Young	$6-$8

Diamond Collection

Troy Aikman	$7-$9
Dan Marino	$8-$10

Barry Sanders	$9-$12

Hockey Bammers

Bear	Price Range
1999 Hockey Bammers	
Sergei Fedorov	$6-$8
Peter Forsberg	$5-$7
Wayne Gretzky	$7-$10
Dominik Hasek	$5-$7
Brett Hull	$5-$7
Jaromir Jagr	$6-$8
Paul Kariya	$5-$7
Eric Lindros	$6-$8
Mark Messier	$5-$7
Patrick Roy	$5-$7
Brendan Shanahan	$7-$10
Steve Yzerman	$7-$10

1999 Bammers Wayne Gretzky.

1999 Bammers Sergei Federov.

Bear	Price Range

1999 Wayne Gretzky Set
Wayne Gretzky with Edmonton Oilers ....$7-$10
Wayne Gretzky with Los Angeles Kings..............$7-$10
Wayne Gretzky with New York Rangers ....$7-$10
Wayne Gretzky with Canada flag,
   Canada exclusive...$14-$20

1999 Figure Skating

Scott Hamilton ....$9-$12

Dorothy Hamill ....$9-$12
Nancy Kerrigan...$9-$12
Tara Lipinski ....$9-$12
Elvis Stojko ....$9-$12
Katarina Witt ....$9-$12

1999 Muhammad Ali Set

Muhammad Ali, bear, gold ....$7-$8
Muhammad Ali, bear, orange
 (Wheaties offer)..$25-$35

Sesame Street Beans

Baby Bear is one of the more popular Sesame Street characters, and he is found in the Sesame Street Beans set. He is very easy to find.

Bear	Price Range
Baby Bear ....$5-$6

Sesame Street Baby Bear.

ShopRite Supermarket bean bag bears.

ShopRite Supermarket

There are six neat little bean bag Teddy Bears named "Scrunchy" in this East Coast-based ShopRite Supermarket set. The purple bear was reportedly made in limited numbers.

Bear	Price Range
Brown with ribbon	$6-$8
Brown with T-shirt	$6-$8
Purple with ribbon	$12-$16
Red with ribbon	$6-$8
Red with T-shirt	$6-$8
Yellow with ribbon	$6-$8

Silver Dollar City Bean Bag Bears

One of the most popular vacation destinations is Branson, Mo. If you or someone you know is going there, look for two sets of Mary Meyer-produced bean bag bears.

Bear	Price Range
"Branson," White Teddy Bear, blue ribbon	$6-$8
"Branson," Brown Teddy Bear, red ribbon	$6-$8
"SDC," White Teddy Bear, red ribbon	$6-$8
"SDC," Brown Teddy Bear, red ribbon	$6-$8

"Silver Dollar City" bean bag bears.

Silver Dollar City "Branson" bean bag bears.

Smokey the Bear

Remember, only you can prevent forest firesÉand collect these bean bags. These are very well done officially licensed Smokey the Bear bean bags. The holiday Smokey has reportedly been limited to between 6,000 and 10,000.

Bear	Price Range
Smokey the Bear	$8-$10
Smokey the Bear, Christmas limited edition	$12-$15

Christmas LE and regular Smokey the Bears.

Snuggle Bean Bag Bear

Snuggle is the advertising bear for Snuggle Fabric Softener. This bean bag version of Snuggle is a true premium, as he was available with the purchase of two jugs of Snuggle.

Bear	Price Range
Snuggle Bear	$8-$12

Snuggle Bear.

Teddy Grahams Bean Bears (bottom): Chunky Chocolate, Chocolatey Chip; (top): Spicey Cinnamon, Yummy Honey.

Teddy Grahams Teddy Bears

Simply put, this one of the best sets of advertising bean bag bears in 1999. About the same size as Beanie Babies, these fellas have great color, are well made and they have bellybuttons! None have hang tags. The offer per-bear is two boxes of Teddy Grahams plus $1 shipping. Do the math–that's eight boxes of Teddy Grahams! Well worth it, though...and the Teddy Grahams aren't bad either!

Bear	Price Range
Chocolatey Chip	$7-$10
Chunky Chocolate	$7-$10
Millennium	$8-$12
Spicey Cinnamon	$7-$10
Yummy Honey	$7-$10

Titanic Bears

Dart Flipcards of Canada has issued two sets of officially licensed Titanic bears that are very popular (I think it was because of some movie or something like that...I just can't put my finger on it!). The R.M.S. Titanic polar bear was available at a nautical exhibit.

Bear	Price Range
Dart Flipcards Series I (15,000 sets)	
Titanic Launched May 31, 1911, white bear	$25-$30
Titanic Lost at Sea, April 15, 1911, blue bear	$25-$30
Dart Flipcards Series II (35,000 sets)	
705 Lost Souls, brown bear	$8-$10
1,503 Lost Souls, blue bear	$8-$10
Captain Smith, white bear with captain's hat	$8-$10
R.M.S. Titanic	
Polar Bear	$8-$10

R.M.S. Titanic Polar Bear.

Travelodge

This sleepy bean bag bear was available at Travelodge hotels.

Bear	Price Range
Travelodge bear	$10-$14

Travelodge bean bag bear.

Ty Beanie Baby Bears

Beanie Baby Bears: What more can be said about Beanie Babies? I think it's all been covered. But just in case you haven't read it yet (yeah, right), I'll reiterate: Beanie Babies are the *crème de la crème* of the bean bag world, the ones who started it all. And the bears are the most popular of the bunch. The colored Teddies are some of the most expensive bean bags on the market. My hat's off to Ty Warner and his wonderful creations. Like everyone else, I look forward to more Beanie Baby bears in the future. Bears marked with an asterisk (*) after "Current" were due to retire by Dec. 31, 1999, according to a statement by Ty Inc.

Beanie Baby Official Club Bears: The Beanie Baby Official Club was started in 1998. Collectors had to purchase the club kit for $10, then send away for a membership card. Once they received the card, collectors could then purchase Clubby (which cost another $10, making the total cost around $20). Collectors liked Clubby, but not the system to get it. In 1999, Ty cleared up the whole situation by including Clubby II with the kit and selling for $20.

Broadway Show Beanie Baby Bears: Special Beanie Baby bears have been for sale at several Broadway Shows in the United States and Canada. Most have a special ribbon with the show's name. These used to be very expensive, but have since fallen back in price, much like the sports events Beanies.

Special Edition Beanie Baby Bears: Some of the most expensive Beanie Baby bears are those given to Ty employees. Very few are made, and very few enter the marketplace. When they do, prices are sky high.

Sports Events Beanie Baby Bears: It wouldn't be baseball season if there weren't Beanie Baby Days at Major League stadiums. Besides baseball, hockey, football and basketball teams have had very large crowds when these special Beanie Babies are handed out. They are usually accompanied by a commemorative card.

Teenie Beanie Baby Bears: This wildly successful McDonald's promotion features small versions of regular Beanie Babies. The 1997 and 1998 promotions featured only one bear–Mel the Koala Bear. The 1999 Teenie Beanie Baby promotion featured a special four-bear set of International Teddys. These Teddys were $2.49 each, on bubble packs with artwork relating to each bear. I expect this same sort of special bear promotion for the year 2000 TBB set. Possible International Bears are Spangle, Osito and Germania.

1997 Teddy the bear.

Beanie Baby Bears

1997 Teddy the bear (R)

Style No. 4200   Date of Birth: Dec. 25, 1996
Released: Sept. 30, 1997   Retired: Dec. 31, 1997

Tag	Price Range
4th	$26-$35
5th	$30-$40

1998 Holiday Teddy (R)

Style No. 4204   Date of Birth: Dec. 25, 1998
Released: Sept. 30, 1998   Retired: Dec. 31, 1998

Tag	Price Range
5th	$40-$50

1999 Holiday Teddy

Style No. 4257   Date of Birth: Dec. 25, 1999
Released: Aug. 31, 1999   Retired: Dec. 31, 1999*

Tag	Price Range
5th	$40-$50

1998 Holiday Teddy.

1999 Signature bear (R)

Style No. 4228   Date of Birth: n/a
Released: Dec. 31, 1998   Retired: Oct. 25, 1999

Tag   **Price Range**
5th ....$11-$18

1999 Signature bear.

Almond the beige bear (R)

Style No. 4246   Date of Birth: Sept. 14, 1999
Released: April 19, 1999   Current*

Tag   **Price Range**
5th ....$8-$14

Almond the beige bear.

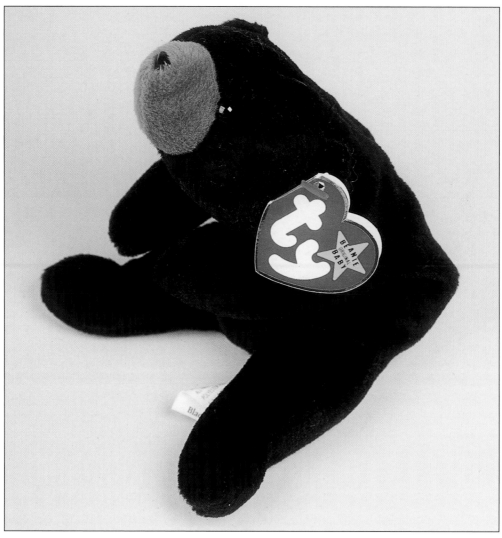

Blackie the bear.

Blackie the bear (R)

Style No. 4011	Date of Birth: July 15, 1994
Released: 1995	Retired: Sept. 15, 1998

Tag	Price Range
1st	$300-$375
2nd	$160-$210
3rd	$45-$75
4th	$9-$12
5th	$7-$10

Britannia the bear (R)
(UK exclusive)

Style No. 4601	Date of Birth: Dec. 15, 1997
Released: Dec. 31, 1997	Retired: July 26, 1999

Tag	Price Range
5th	$80-$120

Chilly the polar bear (R)

Style No. 4012	Date of Birth: n/a
Released: 1994	Retired: 1995

Tag	Price Range
1st	$1,200-$1,500
2nd	$1,100-$1,400
3rd	$550-$850

Cubbie the bear.

Cubbie the bear (R)

Style No. 4010	Date of Birth: Nov. 14, 1996
Released: 1996	Retired: Dec. 31, 1997

1st version: "Brownie" tags

2nd version: "Cubby" tags

Version-Tag	Price Range
1-1st	$2,000-$2,400
2-1st	$500-$650
2-2nd	$250-$425
2-3rd	$90-$160
2-4th	$12-$20
2-5th	$10-$20

Curly the bear.

Curly the bear (R)

Style No. 4052   Date of Birth: April 12, 1996
Released: 1996   Retired: Dec. 31, 1998

Tag	Price Range
4th	$9-$14
5th	$8-$12

Erin the bear (R)

Style No. 4186   Date of Birth: March 17, 1997
Released: Jan. 31, 1998   Retired: May 21, 1999

Tag	Price Range
5th	$10-$14

Erin the bear.

Eucalyptus the koala (R)

Style No. 4240   Date of Birth: April 28, 1999
Released: April 8, 1999   Retired: Oct. 27, 1999

Tag   **Price Range**
5th ....$10-$14

Eucalyptus the koala bear.

Fortune the panda bear (R)

Style No. 4196   Date of Birth: Dec. 6, 1997
Released: May 31, 1998   Retired: Aug. 25, 1999

Tag   **Price Range**
5th ....$7-$10

Fortune the panda bear.

Fuzz the bear.

Fuzz the bear (R)

Style No. 4237   Date of Birth: July 23, 1998
Released: Dec. 31, 1998   Current*

Tag	Price Range
5th	$12-$18

Garcia the bear (R)

Style No. 4051   Date of Birth: Aug. 1, 1995
Released: 1996   Retired: May 11, 1997

Tag	Price Range
3rd	$175-$250
4th	$125-$170

Germania the bear (R)
(Germany exclusive)

Style No. 4236   Date of Birth: Oct. 3, 1998
Released: Dec. 31, 1998   Current*

Tag	Price Range
5th	$150-$225

Garcia the bear.

Glory the bear.

Glory the bear (R)

Style No. 4188   Date of Birth: July 4, 1997
Released: May 31, 1998   Retired: Dec. 31, 1998

Tag   **Price Range**
5th ....$25-$35

Groovy the bear

Style No. 4256   Date of Birth: Jan. 10, 1999
Released: Aug. 31, 1999   Retired: Dec. 31, 1999

Tag   **Price Range**
5th ....$40-$50

Halo the angel bear.

Halo the angel bear (R)

Style No. 4208   Date of Birth: Aug. 31, 1998
Released: Sept. 30, 1998   Current*

Tag	Price Range
5th	$10-$14

Hope the praying bear (R)

Style No. 4223   Date of Birth: March 23, 1998
Released: Dec. 31, 1998   Current*

Tag	Price Range
5th	$10-$15

Hope the praying bear.

Kicks the soccer bear (R)

Style No. 4229   Date of Birth: Aug. 16, 1998
Released: Dec. 31, 1998   Current*

Tag	**Price Range**
5th ....$9-$14	

Kicks the soccer bear.

Libearty the bear (R)

Style No. 4057   Date of Birth: Summer 1996
Released: 1996   Retired: Jan. 1, 1997

Tag	**Price Range**
4th ....$265-$325	

Libearty the bear.

Maple the Canadian bear.

Maple the Canadian bear (R)
(Canada exclusive)

Style No. 4600   Date of Birth: July 1, 1996
Released: Jan. 1, 1997   Retired: July 30, 1999

1st version: "Pride" tags
2nd version: "Maple" tags

Version-Tag	Price Range
1-4th	$325-$400
2-4th	$100-$125
2-5th	$85-$110

Mel the koala bear (R)

Style No. 4162   Date of Birth: 1-15-96
Released: 1-1-97   Retired: 3-31-99

Tag	Price Range
4th	$6-$8
5th	$6-$8

Mel the koala bear.

Millennium the bear (R)

Style No. 4226   Date of Birth: 1-1-99
Released: 12-31-98   Current*

Tag	Price Range
5th	$10-$15

Millennium the bear.

Osito the Mexican bear.

Osito the Mexican bear (R)

Style No. 4244   Date of Birth: Feb. 5, 1999
Released: April 17, 1999   Current*

Tag	Price Range
5th	$18-$25

Peace the tie-dye bear.

Peace the tie-dye bear (R)

Style No. 4053   Date of Birth: Feb. 1, 1996
Released: May 11, 1997   Current*

Tag	Price Range
4th	$13-$20
5th	$10-$14

Pecan the gold bear (R)

Style No. 4251   Date of Birth: April 15, 1999
Released: April 8, 1999   Current*

Tag	Price Range
5th	$10-$14

Peking the panda (R)

Style No. 4013   Date of Birth: n/a
Released: 1994   Retired: 1995

Tag	Price Range
1st	$3,800-$4,300
2nd	$925-$1,400
3rd	$800-$1,200

Pecan the gold bear.

Princess.

Princess (R)

Style No. 4300   Date of Birth: n/a
Released: Oct. 29, 1997   Retired: April 13, 1999

1st version: PVC pellets

2nd version: PE pellets

Version-Tag	Price Range
1-5th	$55-$70
2-5th	$10-$14

Sammy the bear.

Spangle the American bear.

Sammy the bear (R)

Style No. 4215   Date of Birth: June 23, 1998
Released: Dec. 31, 1998   Current*

Tag	Price Range
5th	$8-$10

Spangle the American bear (R)

Style No. 4245   Date of Birth: June 14, 1999
Released: April 24, 1999 Current*

1st version: pink face

2nd version: white face

Version-Tag	Price Range
1-5th	$22-$28
2-5th	$22-$28

Teddy the bear, brown, new face.

Teddy the bear (R)

Brown, new face

Style No. 4050   Date of Birth: Nov. 28, 1995
Released: 1995   Retired: Sept. 30, 1997

Tag	Price Range
2nd	$325-$450
3rd	$250-$325
4th	$70-$90

Teddy the bear (R)

Brown, old face

Style No. 4050   Date of Birth: n/a
Released: 1994   Retired: 1995

Tag	Price Range
1st	$1,450-$1,700
2nd	$1,300-$1,600

Teddy the bear (R)

Cranberry, new face

Style No. 4052   Date of Birth: n/a
Released: 1995   Retired: 1995

Tag	Price Range
2nd	$1,800-$2,000
3rd	$1,600-$1,800

Teddy the bear (R)

Cranberry, old face

Style No. 4052   Date of Birth: n/a
Released: 1994   Retired: 1995

Tag	Price Range
1st	$1,700-$1,850
2nd	$1,400-$1,600

Teddy the bear (R)

Jade, new face

Style No. 4057   Date of Birth: n/a
Released: 1995   Retired: 1995

Tag	Price Range
2nd	$1,100-$1,300
3rd	$1,000-$1,200

Teddy the bear (R)

Jade, old face

Style No. 4057   Date of Birth: n/a
Released: 1994   Retired: 1995

Tag	Price Range
1st	$1,000-$1,200
2nd	$900-$1,000

Teddy the bear (R)

Magenta, new face

Style No. 4056   Date of Birth: n/a
Released: 1995   Retired: 1995

Tag	Price Range
2nd	$1,150-$1,400
3rd	$1,000-$1,200

Teddy the bear (R)

Magenta, old face

Style No. 4056   Date of Birth: n/a
Released: 1994   Retired: 1995

Tag	Price Range
1st	$1,100-$1,300
2nd	$1,000-$1,200

Teddy the bear (R)

Teal, new face

Style No. 4051   Date of Birth: n/a
Released: 1995   Retired: 1995

Tag	Price Range
2nd	$1,150-$1,300
3rd	$1,000-$1,200

Teddy the bear (R)

Teal, old face

Style No. 4051   Date of Birth: n/a
Released: 1994   Retired: 1995

Tag	Price Range
1st	$1,100-$1,400
2nd	$1,000-$1,200

Teddy the bear (R)

Violet, new face

Style No. 4055   Date of Birth: n/a
Released: 1995   Retired: 1995

Tag	Price Range
2nd	$1,200-$1,400
3rd	$1,100-$1,300

Teddy the bear (R)

Violet, old face

Style No. 4055   Date of Birth: n/a
Released: 1994   Retired: 1995

Tag	Price Range
1st	$1,250-$1,400
2nd	$1,200-$1,400

New face and old face comparison.

Teddy the bear, Violet, old face.

Valentina the bear (R)

Style No. 4233   Date of Birth: Feb. 14, 1998
Released: Dec. 31, 1998   Retired: Dec. 31, 1999

Tag	Price Range
5th	$8-$12

Valentino the bear (R)

Style No. 4058   Date of Birth: Feb. 14, 1994
Released: 1995   Retired: Dec. 31, 1998

Tag	Price Range
2nd	$275-$400
3rd	$120-$140
4th	$10-$18
5th	$9-$14

Valentina the bear.

The End the bear

Style No. 4265   Date of Birth: n/a
Released: Aug. 31, 1999   Retired: Dec. 31, 1999*

Tag	Price Range
5th	$40-$50

Ty 2K the bear

Style No. 4262   Date of Birth: Jan. 1, 2000
Released: Aug. 31, 1999   Retired: Dec. 31, 1999*

Tag	Price Range
5th	$40-$50

Wallace the bear

Style No. 4264   Date of Birth: Jan. 25, 1999
Released: Aug. 31, 1999   Retired: Dec. 31, 1999*

Tag	Price Range
5th	$30

Valentino the bear.

Clubby.

Broadway Show Beanie Baby Bears

Bear	Price Range
Fosse	
Valentino	$20-$28
Joseph and the Amazing Technicolor Dreamcoat	
Garcia	$175-$200
Peace	$25-$32
Livent	
Blackie	$18-$25
Hope	$20-$30
Maple	$90-$130
Phantom of the Opera	
Fortune	$28-$40
Maple	$250-$300
Ragtime	
Curly (burgundy, ivory or navy ribbon), each	$20-$25
Glory	$50-$60
Signature Bear (burgundy or ivory ribbon), each	$20-$30
Teddy, NF brown	$125-$175

Special Edition Beanie Baby Bears

Bear	Price Range
#1 Bear, Ty Representative Bear	$4,000-$5,000
Billionaire Bear #1, green, Ty Employee Bear	$3,000-$4,000
Billionaire Bear #2, magenta, Ty Employee Bear	$3,000-$3,500
Curly, Toys for Tots, Fall 1998	$35-$45
Maple, Special Olympics	$150-$175
Teddy, violet, NF, green bow, Ty Employee Bear	$1,500-$2,000
Teddy, violet, NF, red bow, Ty Employee Bear	$1,500-$2,000
Valentino, Special Olympics, July 1998	$40-$50
Valentino, Toys for Tots, March 1998	$40-$50

Beanie Baby Official Club Bears

Bear	Price Range
Clubby, 1998	$30-$40
Clubby II, 1999	$18-$25

Clubby II.

Sports Events Beanie Baby Bears

Baseball

Bear	Price Range
1997	
Chicago Cubs, Cubbie, 5-18-97	$60-$75
1998	
All Star Game, Glory, 7-7-98	$80-$100
Chicago Cubs Convention, Cubbie	$300-$350
New York Mets, Curly, 8-22-98	$30-$40
New York Yankees, Valentino, 5-17-98	$120-$150
1999	
Chicago Cubs Convention, Cubbie	$125-$175
Chicago Cubs, Erin, 8-5-99	$30-$35
Chicago Cubs, Millennium, 9-26-99	$30-$35
Chicago Cubs, Sammy, 4-25-99	$30-$40
Kansas City Royals, Fortune, 6-6-99	$15-$20
New York Mets, Valentina	$35-$40
New York Yankees, Millennium	$38-$42
New York Yankees, Signature Bear	$30-$35
Oakland A's, Peace, 5-1-99	$22-$26

Basketball

	Price Range
1998	
NBA: San Antonio Spurs, Curly, 4-27-98	$50-$60
WNBA: Charlotte Sting, Curly, 6-15-98	$30-$40
WNBA: Cleveland Rockers, Curly, 8-15-98	$30-$35

Chicago Cubs, Cubbie, 5-18-97 (the first Beanie Baby sports promotion).

Football

Bear	Price Range
1998	
Chicago Bears Kids Club, Blackie, 7-98	$20-$25
Chicago Bears, Blackie, 11-8-98	$30-$35
Chicago Bears, Curly, 12-20-98	$30-$40

Hockey

Bear	Price Range
1998	
Boston Bruins, Blackie, 10-12-98	$35-$45

New York Yankees, Valentino, 5-17-98 (David Wells threw a perfect game for the Yanks that day!).

The four International Teenie Beanie bears with their packages: Glory, Brittania, Maple and Erin.

Teenie Beanie Baby Bears

Bear	Price Range
1998 Set	
Mel the Koala Bear	$2-$3
1999 Set	
Britannia the English Bear	$3-$5
Erin the Irish Bear	$3-$5
Glory the U.S. Bear	$3-$5
Glory the U.S. Bear, employee version	$15-$25
Maple the Canadian Bear	$3-$5

Ty Attic Treasures® Bears

Ty is on a winning streak that just doesn't end! Its Beanie Baby and Beanie Buddy lines are two of the hottest in the country, and its bear-heavy Attic Treasures line is doing just fine. The first Attics showed up in 1993, around the same time that Beanie Babies arrived. Like the early Beanie Babies, Attics lingered in gift shops with few takers. Ty stuck with the Attics, discontinuing (retiring) characters, while adding new characters and changing their looks (mostly by giving them clothing in 1997). When Beanie Babies hit the big time in 1996 and 1997, collectors began to recognize the quality, diversity and collectibility of the Attics line. Since then, Attics have drawn in thousands of new collectors, and it appears that this Ty series is one that will remain popular for years to come.

The appeal of the Attic bears is mostly due to their look and feel of quality. Measuring from 6 inches to 16 inches tall, they convey a striking, old-style appearance. They're jam-packed with personality, much more than Beanie Babies, in my estimation. With their serious faces, they look like they could have been made in the early part of this century. Attics were no doubt inspired by the German company Steiff, which began producing jointed bears in 1902.

Since the Attics are jointed in their necks, arms and legs, they can be posed in various ways, and they look great on shelves or in display cases. Current Attics are very inexpensive, usually $6-$7 for the small bears and $10-$12 for the large bears. Also, Attic collectors can generally get the new Attic issues fairly quickly and at retail price, especially compared to getting new Beanie Babies. It's a less stressful pursuit than trying to track down Beanies.

Of more than 100 different Attic characters, about two-thirds are bears (Teddy bears, panda bears, polar bears, koala bears and pot-bellied bears). *Note: Woolie Brown was never produced for sale. There are reportedly a few prototypes.* Many of the bears are "related" to each other in one form or another. For instance, there are sisters (Emily, Nola & Rebecca, Abby and Cassie), brothers and sisters (Oscar and Abby, Cassie and Barry, Chelsea and Fraser), and brothers (Clyde and Cody, Checkers and Domino, Boris and Ivan).

The bears have changed mightily since they were first issued. From 1993-1996, the bears were naked, except for neck ribbons or head bows. Since 1996, most of the bears have been clothed. Oftentimes, there are at least two variations of a bear: for example, Emily with a

bow and Emily with a hat and dress; Cassanova with a neck ribbon and Cassanova with a sweater. "No clothes" usually means a higher value, due to the earlier tag. Bears issued in the last two years have had elaborate costumes. Ty produced two exclusive bears (in the same style as

Grant): Jack (British flag) and Mackenzie (Canada flag). Since they are available in those countries, they are both in demand.

Hang tags: Attics have undergone hang tag-style changes just as Beanie Babies have. The red tags are made of the same material as Beanie tags; the beige tags are thin and bendable and do not show wear or damage as easily as the red tags. So far, there have been seven different styles of hang tags:

1st style: Red tag, two-sided heart with "ty" in thin letters
2nd style: Red tag, same front as first, now a fold-out tag
3rd style: Red tag, fat "ty" letters
4th style: Red tag, fat letters, green "Collectible" banner
5th style: Tan tag, maroon "ty" with "Collectible" banner
6th style: Same as 5th, but "Comic" font
7th style: Red tag, same as 3rd, but the inside has a one-line saying (Peter the pumpkin bear, it says: "Trick or Treat"). The 3rd tags do not have a saying.

Buttons: When Ty dressed the naked Attic bears, some had buttons added to their outfits, usually two buttons on the outer side of the chest. Ty decided to remove the buttons from the bears' clothes in 1997 (some believe that the buttons were removed because they were a potential choking hazard, though nothing is confirmed). When Ty did this, many Attics had their buttons physically removed, thus causing holes in the outfits, so if you run across an Attic with holes in its clothes, this is likely what happened. Since there were many fewer Attics with buttons than without, the button versions are more highly valued.

Internet sites: To learn more about Attics, visit the excellent "Kim 'n Kevin's Collectibles" internet site at *www.knkcollectibles.com*. Mary Catherine Cochran and Terri Siegel operate a Ty Attic-only Internet site called "Maison D'Ours" at *www.maisondours.com*. Ty's site, *www.ty.com*, has information on new Attics and retirees, plus a list of current and retired Attics.

Abby.

Abby (R)

Retired: 1998

Hang tag/attire	Price Range
2nd, burgundy ribbon	$70-$85
3rd, burgundy ribbon	$45-$55
4th, burgundy overalls	$30-$40
5th, burgundy overalls with rose	$20-$25
5th, burgundy overalls	$15-$20
6th, burgundy overalls	$10-$12

Allura.

Allura (R)

Current

Hang tag/attire	Price Range
7th, red swimsuit and life preserver	$6-$8

Azure (R)

Current

Hang tag/attire	Price Range
7th, blue silky ribbon	$6-$8

Azure

Barry (R)

Retired: 1997

Hang tag/attire	Price Range
5th, burgundy and blue vest	$80-$100

Beargundy

Current

Hang tag/attire	Price Range
7th	$10-$13

Barry.

Bearington.

Bearington (R)

Retired: 1998

Hang tag/attire	Price Range
6th, blue plaid bow	$10-$13

Bearkhardt

Current

Hang tag/attire	Price Range
7th	$10-$13

Beezee (R)

Current

Hang tag/attire	Price Range
7th, black and yellow bee outfit	$6-$8

Beezee.

Bluebeary.

Bluebeary (R)

Retired: 1999

Hang tag/attire	Price Range
6th, blue ribbon	$7-$10
7th, blue ribbon	$7-$10

Boris.

Boris (R)

Retired: 1997

Hang tag/attire	Price Range
5th, green, red and blue sweater vest	$30-$40

Breezy (R)

Current

Hang tag/attire	Price Range
7th, blue and white dress, blue bow	$6-$8

Breezy.

Brisbane (R)

Current

Hang tag/attire	Price Range
7th, no attire	$6-$8

Brisbane.

Bugsy.

Bugsy (R)

Retired: July 28, 1999

Hang tag/attire	Price Range
7th, ladybug outfit	$6-$8

Carlton (R)

Retired: 1997

Hang tag/attire	Price Range
5th, light blue overalls	$30-$40

Carlton

Cassanova.

Cassanova (R)

Retired: 1999

Hang tag/attire	Price Range
6th, white sweater with red heart	$7-$10
7th, white sweater with red heart	$7-$10

Cassie.

Cassie (R)

Retired: 1997

Hang tag/attire	Price Range
2nd, burgundy ribbon	$100-$120
3rd, burgundy ribbon	$50-$60
4th, burgundy ribbon	$40-$50
5th, blue jumper, blue bow in hair	$20-$30

Charles (R)

Retired: 1997

Hang tag/attire	Price Range
5th, burgundy overalls	$40-$50

Charles.

Checkers (R)

Retired: 1997

Hang tag/attire	Price Range
2nd, no attire	$65-$85
3rd, no attire	$50-$60
4th, no attire	$35-$45
5th, no attire	$7-$10
5th, burgundy sweater	$8-$12
6th, no attire	$6-$8

Checkers.

Chelsea.

Chelsea (R)

Retired: 1998

Hang tag/attire	Price Range
5th, beige and burgundy sweater	$8-$12
6th, beige and burgundy sweater	$7-$10

Christopher (R)

Retired: 1998

Hang tag/attire	Price Range
5th, blue corduroy overalls, gold buttons	$12-$16
5th, blue corduroy overalls	$8-$12
6th, blue corduroy overalls	$7-$10

Christopher.

Clyde.

Copperfield.

Clifford (R)

Retired: 1996

Hang tag/attire	Price Range
1st, hump back, green ribbon	$250-$325
1st, straight back, green ribbon	$200-$250

Clyde (R)

Retired: 1997

Hang tag/attire	Price Range
5th, burgundy sweater	$30-$40

Cody.

Cody (R)

Current

Hang tag/attire	Price Range
2nd, no attire	$60-$75
3rd, no attire	$45-$60
4th, no attire	$30-$40
5th, no attire	$8-$12
6th, no attire	$6-$8
7th, no attire	$6-$8

Copperfield (R)

Retired: 1997

Hang tag/attire	Price Range
5th, blue and white sweater	$40-$50

Dexter (R)

Retired: 1997

Hang tag/attire	Price Range
1st, burgundy ribbon	$65-$85
2nd, burgundy ribbon	$50-$60
3rd, burgundy ribbon	$40-$50
4th, burgundy ribbon	$30-$40
5th, red and white overalls, burgundy ribbon	$14-$18

Dickens (R)

Retired: 1998

Hang tag/attire	Price Range
4th, no attire	$30-$40
5th, burgundy overalls	$8-$12
6th, no attire	$7-$10

Dexter.

Left: Dickens 6th; right, Dickens 5th.

Digby.

Emily.

Digby (R)

Retired: 1997

Hang tag/attire	Price Range
1st, hump back, green ribbon	$175-$225
1st, straight back, green ribbon	$140-$175
4th, green ribbon	$60-$75
5th, red, white and blue USA sweater	$50-$60

Domino.

Domino (R)

Retired: 1997

Hang tag/attire	Price Range
5th, lavender overalls with buttons	$35-$45
5th, lavender overalls	$25-$30

Emily (R)

Retired: 1997

Hang tag/attire	Price Range
1st, green head bow and large feet	$125-$150
1st, green head bow	$100-$125
2nd, green head bow	$80-$100
3rd, green head bow	$65-$85
4th, green head bow	$60-$75
5th, green head bow	$50-$65
5th, red floral hat and dress	$45-$60

Esmerelda (R)

Retired: 1998

Hang tag/attire	Price Range
6th, witch hat and cape	$8-$12
7th, witch hat and cape	$7-$10

Esmerelda.

Eve.

Eve (R)

Current

Hang tag/attire	Price Range
6th, white lace cape, flowers on head	$8-$12
7th, white lace cape, flowers on head	$8-$12

Fairbanks (R)

Current

Hang tag/attire	Price Range
7th, blue and red sweater	$6-$8

Fairbanks.

Fraser.

Fraser (R)

Retired: 1998

Hang tag/attire	Price Range
1st, artist name on tags, green ribbon	$200-$225
1st, green ribbon	$150-$175
2nd, green ribbon	$65-$85
3rd, green ribbon	$40-$50
4th, green ribbon	$30-$40
5th, blue and white sweater	$8-$12
6th, blue and white sweater	$7-$10

Frederick.

Frederick (R)

Retired: 1997

Hang tag/attire	Price Range
5th, red and blue sweater	$35-$45

Gem (R)

Retired: 1999

Hang tag/attire	Price Range
7th, maroon robe	$10-$13

Gem.

Gilbert (R)

Retired: 1997

Hang tag/attire	Price Range
1st, white with red ribbon	$225-$275
1st, gold with red ribbon	$135-$175
5th, gold, denim overalls with gold buttons	$12-$16
5th gold, denim overalls	$8-$12

Gilbert.

Gordon.

Gordon (R)

Current

Hang tag/attire	Price Range
7th, yellow raincoat and hat	$10-$12

Grady (R)

Retired: 1997

Hang tag/attire	Price Range
* 5th, green, blue and rust sweater vest	$60-$75

* Grady is exactly the same as Grover "Gold," except for his hang tag

Grant (R)

Retired: Aug. 30, 1999

Hang tag/attire	Price Range
6th, blue sweater with U.S. flag	$10-$12
7th, blue sweater with U.S. flag	$10-$12

Grant.

Left: Grover "Gold" (no tag) 4th; right: Grover "Gold" 5th.

Grover "Gold" (R)

Retired: 1997

Hang tag/attire	Price Range
4th, blue ribbon	$65-$85
5th, green sweater vest	$18-$25

Grover "Brown" (R)

16-inch retired: 1997

Hang tag/attire	Price Range
2nd, 16-inch, green ribbon	$60-$75
3rd, 16-inch, green ribbon	$75-$90
4th, 16-inch, green ribbon	$30-$35
5th, 16-inch, green overalls with gold buttons	$18-$25
5th, 16-inch, green overalls	$14-$18

Left: Grover "Brown" with ribbon (no hang tag); right: Grover "Brown" 5th.

Grover "Brown" (R)

13-inch retired: 1998

Hang tag/attire	Price Range
6th, 13-inch, green overalls	$14-$18

Gwyndolyn

Current

Hang tag/attire	Price Range
7th	$10-$13

Grover "Brown" 13-inch.

Heartley.

Heartley (R)

Current

Hang tag/attire	Price Range
7th, white sweater with hearts	$10-$12

Henry (R)

Henry "Gold" Retired: 1994
Henry "Brown" Retired: 1997

Hang tag/attire	Price Range
1st, "Gold," blue ribbon	$325-$400
1st, "Brown," blue ribbon	$90-$110
5th, "Brown," green overalls with gold buttons	$20-$25
5th, "Brown," green overalls	$12-$16

Henry.

Isabella.

Jangle.

Isabella (R)

Current

Hang tag/attire	Price Range
7th, leopard-print hat and coat	$10-$12

Ivan.

Ivan (R)

Retired: July 13, 1999

Hang tag/attire	Price Range
2nd, no attire	$65-$75
3rd, no attire	$40-$55
4th, no attire	$25-$35
5th, no attire	$7-$10
6th, no attire	$6-$8
7th, no attire	$5-$7

Jack (R) (UK exclusive)

Current

Hang tag/attire	Price Range
6th, white sweater with British flag	$30-$40
7th, white sweater with British flag	$20-$25

Jangle (R)

Current

Hang tag/attire	Price Range
7th, red and white stocking hat, red scarf	$7-$10

Laurel (R)

Retired: 1998

Hang tag/attire	Price Range
7th, red collar	$7-$10

Mackenzie (R) (Canada exclusive)

Current

Hang tag/attire	Price Range
6th, white sweater with Canada flag	$55-$70
7th, white sweater with Canada flag	$30-$40

Laurel.

Malcolm.

Malcolm (R)

Retired: 1997

Hang tag/attire	Price Range
2nd, blue ribbon	$80-$100
4th, blue sweater with red and white stripes	$45-$60
5th, blue sweater with red and white stripes	$30-$40

Malcolm (R) (guard uniform)

Current

Hang tag/attire	Price Range
7th, British guard uniform	$10-$13

Malcolm (guard uniform).

Mason.

Nola.

Mason (R)

Retired: 1998

Hang tag/attire	Price Range
2nd, burgundy ribbon	$60-$75
3rd, burgundy ribbon	$50-$65
4th, burgundy ribbon	$30-$40
5th, green and white sweater	$10-$15
6th, green and white sweater	$8-$12

Nicholas.

Nicholas (R)

Retired: 1998

Hang tag/attire	Price Range
1st, red ribbon	$150-$200
4th, red ribbon	$90-$125
5th, red sweater with white heart	$10-$15
6th, red sweater with white heart	$8-$12

Nola (R)

Retired: 1997

Hang tag/attire	Price Range
1st, pink neck ribbon	$125-$150
1st, pink head bow	$100-$120
2nd, pink head bow	$80-$100
3rd, pink head bow	$80-$100
4th, pink head bow	$80-$100
5th, pink floral hat and dress	$65-$85

Orion

Current

Hang tag/attire	Price Range
7th	$10-$13

Oscar (R)

Retired: 1998

Hang tag/attire	Price Range
2nd, blue ribbon	$50-$65
3rd, blue ribbon	$30-$40
4th, green corduroy overalls	$25-$35
5th, green corduroy overalls	$10-$15
6th, green corduroy overalls	$8-$12

Oscar.

Peppermint.

Peppermint (R)

Retired: July 13, 1999

Hang tag/attire	Price Range
6th, red hat and scarf	$6-$8
7th, red hat and scarf	$6-$8

Peter (R)

Retired: 1998

Hang tag/attire	Price Range
6th, pumpkin belly and hat	$7-$10
7th, pumpkin belly and hat	$7-$10

Peter.

Left: Picadilly 7th; right: Picadilly 6th.

Precious.

Picadilly (R)

Current

Hang tag/attire	Price Range
6th, blue and green outfit, "Small Bear" tag	$7-$10
6th, blue and green outfit, "Picadilly" tag	$7-$10
7th, blue, green, red, orange outfit	$6-$8

Precious (R)

Retired: 1998

Hang tag/attire	Price Range
6th, sleeping hat, diaper and pillow	$10-$13

Rafaella (R)

Current

Hang tag/attire	**Price Range**
7th, wings, antennas, purple and pink flowers on head	$7-$10

Rafaella.

Rebecca.

Rebecca (R)

Retired: 1997

Hang tag/attire	**Price Range**
2nd, blue head bow	$80-$95
4th, blue head bow	$60-$75
5th, red checker head bow, blue overalls	$50-$65

Reggie.

Reggie (R)

Retired: 1993

Hang tag/attire	**Price Range**
1st, blue ribbon	$175-$225

Rosalie (R)

Current

Hang tag/attire	**Price Range**
7th, white floral dress, pink flower bonnet	$6-$8

Rosalie.

Salty (R)

Current

Hang tag/attire	**Price Range**
7th, blue sweater with anchor	$6-$8

Salty.

Samuel (R)

Current

Hang tag/attire	**Price Range**
6th, blue coat, striped pants and hat, "Large Bear" tag	$12-$16
6th, blue coat, striped pants and hat, "Samuel" tag	$10-$13
7th, blue coat, striped pants and hat	$10-$13

Samuel.

Scotch.

Scotch (R)

Retired: 1998

Hang tag/attire	**Price Range**
6th, red plaid hat and overalls	$10-$13

Skylar (R)

Retired: 1999

Hang tag/attire	**Price Range**
7th, light blue sweater	$7-$9

Spruce

Current

Hang tag/attire	**Price Range**
7th	$10-$13

Skylar.

Sterling with small wings at left; large wings at right.

Sterling (R)

Retired: May 24, 1999

Hang tag/attire	**Price Range**
7th, silver wings and head bow (large wings).....$7-$10	
7th, silver wings and head bow (small wings)....$7-$10	

Susannah (R)

Current

Hang tag/attire	**Price Range**
7th, white floral dress, yellow flower bonnet........$6-$8	

Susannah.

Tiny Tim with buttons at left; without buttons at right.

Tiny Tim (R)

Retired: 1997

Hang tag/attire	Price Range
1st, burgundy ribbon	$110-$140
2nd, burgundy ribbon	$55-$70
4th, burgundy ribbon	$35-$45
5th, red and white pinstripe overalls, red buttons	$12-$16
5th, red and white pinstripe overalls	$10-$15

Tyler (R)

Retired: 1996

Hang tag/attire	Price Range
1st, hump back, burgundy ribbon	$90-$110
1st, straight back, burgundy ribbon	$85-$100
2nd, straight back, burgundy ribbon	$50-$65
4th, straight back, rust sweater	$35-$50
5th, straight back, rust sweater	$25-$35

Tyler.

Tyrone.

Watson (note buttons).

Tyra

Retired: Oct. 19, 1999

Hang tag/attire	Price Range
7th	$10-$13

Tyrone (R)

Current

Hang tag/attire	Price Range
7th, red smoking jacket	$10-$13

Watson (R)

Retired: 1997

Hang tag/attire	Price Range
5th, red, blue and white checker overalls, red buttons	$25-$35
5th, red, blue and white checker overalls	$20-$30

Wee Willie with buttons at left; without buttons at right.

William.

Wee Willie (R)

Retired: 1997

Hang tag/attire	Price Range
2nd, green ribbon, "Wee Willie" tag	$60-$80
2nd, green ribbon, "Wee Willie" tag	$60-$80
5th, denim overalls, baseball buttons	$15-$22
5th, denim overalls	$10-$13

William (R)

Current

Hang tag/attire	Price Range
7th, black pinstripe shirt and pants	$10-$13

Woolie "Gold" (R)

Retired: 1993

Hang tag/attire	Price Range
1st, red ribbon	$300-$400

Beanie Buddy Chilly.

Ty Beanie Buddy® Bears

Ty's Beanie Buddies have been a big hit from their introduction in 1998. Most popular are the bears, of course, as far as collectors are concerned. These large versions of Beanie Babies sell for a very affordable price of around $10 when you can find them on the retail level. The Teddy Bears are very hard to locate at the retail shops for retail price. The Buddies look great when displayed with their smaller counterparts.

Beanie Buddy Peking.

Beanie Buddy Erin.

Beanie Buddy Millennium.

Beanie Buddy Cranberry Teddy.

Bear	Price Range
Britannia the Bear	$40-$60
Chilly the Polar Bear	$12-$16
Erin the Teddy	$25-$35
Fuzz the Teddy	$40-$50
Halo the Bear	$20-$30
Maple the Bear	$35-$45
Hope the Praying Bear	$16-$22
Millennium the Y2K Bear	$35-$45
Peace the Bear	$20-$30
Spangle the Bear	$20-$30
Peking the Panda Bear	$12-$16
Princess the Lady Di Bear	$40-$50
Teddy (Cranberry)	$20-$30

Ty Plush® Bears

The "plush" line of collectibles from Ty was introduced in 1993 and seemingly discontinued in 1998, as there have been few "traditional" plush released since then. While the line has been discontinued, there are still a lot of people interested in the line and in the bears. What follows is a price list for the some of more popular and frequently found Ty Plush bears. There are some extremely rare bears that are hardly ever offered for sale. For more information about Ty Plush, visit "Kim Ôn Kevin's Collectibles" internet site at *www.knkcollectibles.com.*

Bear	Price Range
1997 Holiday Bear	$18-$24
Arctic the Polar Bear	$35-$50
Aurora the Polar Bear	$20-$25
Baby Cinnamon	$20-$30
Baby Curly	$9-$12
Baby Ginger	$12-$16
Baby Paws, black	$9-$12
Baby Paws, brown	$9-$12
Baby Paws, white	$9-$12
Baby PJ, brown	$12-$16
Baby PJ, white	$30-$40
Baby Powder	$9-$12
Baby Spice	$9-$12

Baby Curly.

Bailey	$20-$30
Bamboo the Panda	$9-$12
Baron	$50-$60
Bluebeary	$12
Brownie	$30-$40
Butterbeary	$12
Cinnamon, #5021	$25-$35
Cocoa	$9-$12
Curly	$20-$30
Cuzzy	$30-$40
Dumpling Brown	$20-$30
Dumpling White	$20-$30
Eleanor	$30-$40
Faith	$18-$24
Forest	$12-$16
Baron	$50-$60
Brownie	$30-$40
Cinnamon, #5021	$25-$35
Cocoa	$9-$12
Curly	$20-$30
Cuzzy	$30-$40
Dumpling Brown	$20-$30
Dumpling White	$20-$30
Eleanor	$30-$40
Faith	$18-$24
Forest	$12-$16
Fuzzy	$30-$40

Cocoa.

McGee.

Magee.

Ginger	$20-$30
Honey	$20-$30
Hope	$14-$18
Lazy	$16-$22
McGee	$20-$30
Magee	$10-$12
Mandarin the Panda	$40-$50
Midnight, #5101	$30-$40
Nutmeg	$30-$40
Oreo the Panda, #5010	$65-$80
Oreo the Panda, #5013	$25-$35
Paws Black	$20-$30
Paws Brown	$20-$30
Paws White	$20-$30
P.J. Brown	$20-$25
P.J. White	$50-$60
Powder	$20-$25
Prayer Bear Gold, #5600	$140-$175
Prayer Bear White, #5601	$125-$150
Purplebeary	$12
Rags	$20-$30
Romeo	$10-$15
Romeo, gold ribbon	$10-$15
Romeo, Mother's Day	$10-$15
Ruffles	$35-$50
Rufus	$30-$40
Rumples Beige	$20-$30
Rumples Gold	$20-$30
Sam	$100-$150
Scruffy Gold, #5013	$50-$60
Shadow	$30-$40

Shaggy Beige	$50-$60
Shaggy Brown	$50-$60
Shaggy Gold	$50-$60
Sugar, #5007	$30-$40
Theodore	$40-$50
Vanilla	$50-$65
Wuzzy	$30-$40
Yukon	$25-$35

Romeo, Mother's Day.

TVBBC Buckingham Palace, Beefeater and British Bobby.

Velveteen Bean Bear Company

Three of the finest bean bags you'll ever see are from England, courtesy of The Velveteen Bean Bear Company (TVBBC). These beautiful bears were designed by Tina Watson. They are not often found for sale.

Bear	Price Range
Beefeater bear	$18-$22
British Bobby bear	$18-$22
Buckingham Palace bear	$18-$22

Walker's 50th Birthday Bean Bear

This advertising bear from Great Britain was produced for Walker's Crisps (potato chips) for the 50th anniversary of Walker's. Collectors in Great Britain had to send in proof of purchases to get this bear, so they are not easy to find.

Bear	Price Range
Walker's 50th Birthday Bear	$12-$16

Walker's 50th Birthday Bean Bear.

Union Pacific Railroad Bean Bag Bear

This adorable little bean bag bear with the Union Pacific logo on its chest was available from the Union Pacific website at *www.uprr.com/uprr/retail* or through the company's store catalog.

Bear	Price Range
Union Pacific Bear, blue	$6-$8
Union Pacific Bear, red	$6-$8
Union Pacific Bear, white	$15-$18

Union Pacific Railroad Bean Bag Bear.

U.S. Open Golf Bean Bag Bear.

U.S. Open Golf Bean Bag Bear

This bean bag bear was sold at the 1998 U.S. Open Golf Tournament in San Francisco. It has "U.S. Open, The Olympic Club, 1998" embroidered on its chest. I have heard reports that only about 2,000 of these bears were made, but I cannot confirm that.

Bear	Price Range
U.S. Open Golf Bean Bag Bear	$18-$22

Winnie the Pooh Bean Bags

Disney's first animated treatment of Winnie the Pooh was in the 1966 cartoon called "Winnie the Pooh and the Honey Tree." He has gone on to become one of Disney's most popular characters in merchandise. Pooh is one of the stars in the Disney Mini Bean Bag Plush line.

There are many people outside the bean bag collecting community who specialize in Pooh, so that's one reason his bean bags are so popular. Gund and Mattel/Fisher-Price have also produced some bean bag Poohs.

Disney Pooh Bumblebee.

Disney Pooh Choo-Choo.

Winnie the Pooh
Disney Mini Bean Bag Plush

Bear	Price Range
As Eeyore (LE 1999, catalog exclusive)	$9-$12
As Tigger (LE 1999)	$8-$10
Baseball Pooh	$7-$9
Bumblebee Pooh	$7-$9
Choo-Choo Pooh (R)	$7-$9
Classic Pooh (R)	$6-$8
Christmas Pooh (green scarf, LE 1997)	$25-$32
Easter Pooh, lavender bunny suit (DST only, LE 1998)	$65-$80
Easter Pooh, red shirt, bunny ears (LE 1998)	$30-$40
Easter Bunny Pooh, blue (LE 1999)	$12-$16
Easter Bunny Pooh, white (LE 1999, Japan Exclusive)	$20-$25
Fishing Pooh	$6-$8
Flower Pooh (a.k.a. "Mother's Day Pooh") (R)	$14-$18
Friendship Pooh (LE 1999)	$26-$30
Gradnite Pooh, DL (LE 1998)	$22-$26
Gradnite Pooh, WDW (floral shorts, LE 1998)	$25-$30

Hanukkah Pooh (LE 1998) ....$10-$12
Jumping Bean Pooh..$8-$10
Nautical Pooh ....$7-$9
Picnic Pooh (R) ....$8-$10
Pilot Pooh (R)..$7-$9
Pumpkin Pooh (LE 1998) ....$10-$13
Santa Pooh V1 (hard nose, LE 1997) ....$20-$25
Santa Pooh V2 (stitched nose, LE 1997) ....$16-$20

Snowflake Sweater Pooh (LE 1998)........................$25-$32
Snowman Pooh (LE 1998) ....$12-$15
Test Pooh (footpads, hard nose) (R) ....$20-$25
V2 Pooh (no footpads, hard nose) (R) ....$8-$12
V3 Pooh (no footpads, stitched nose) (R) ....$6-$8
Valentine Pooh (LE 1998) ....$50-$60
Christmas (green scarf, LE 1997) ....$14-$20
With red sweater (LE 1999) ....$10-$14

Disney Pooh Santa: (from left) Santa V2, Santa V1 and Christmas.

Disney · Pooh regular versions: V1 (test), V3, V2.

*Disney Pooh
Easter: (from left)
with ears and
in lavender
bunny suit.*

Disney Pooh Classic.

Disney Pooh Easter: (from left) blue suit and white suit.

Disney Pooh Gradnite: (from left) without shorts and with shorts.

Disney Pooh Hanukkah.

Disney Pooh Flower.

Disney Pooh Pilot.

Disney Pooh Pumpkin.

Disney Pooh Snowflake Sweater.

Disney Pooh Snowman.

Left: Disney Pooh Red Heart Sweater; right: Disney Pooh Valentine.

Winnie the Pooh Gund Bean Bag

<u>Bear</u>	<u>Price</u>
<u>Range</u>	
Classic Pooh..$6-$8	

Gund Classic Pooh.

Mattel/Fisher Price
Winnie the Pooh Bean Bags

Bear Range	Price
Easter Pooh-Rade, 1999, boxed set	$10-$12
Halloween, 1999, boxed set	$10-$12
Nature Lovin' Pooh & Friends, boxed set	$13-$16
Pooh, Santa hat, Winnie the Pooh Beanbag Friends Holiday 1998	$6-$8
Pooh, small, velcro on paws	$4-$5
Pooh, Starbeans hang tag, various outfits	$4-$5
Pooh, Winnie the Pooh Beanbag Friends	$4-$5

Easter Pooh-Rade.

Nature Lovin' Pooh & Friends.

Yogi Bear & Boo Boo

Yogi Bear will turn 40 in the year 2000, as this picnic-basket thief debuted in 1960. Yogi was found in a Cartoon Network set that was available at Target Stores in 1998. The original retail price was $2.99. This Yogi is average quality, but not commonly found. Warner Brothers also came out with a Yogi, plus his little buddy Boo Boo.

Bear	Price Range
Boo Boo, Warner	$9-$11
Yogi Bear, Cartoon Network	$9-$11
Yogi Bear, Warner	$7-$8

Cartoon Network Yogi Bear.

Warner Brothers Boo-Boo and Yogi.

The Cats

I must have more than 100 cats...not real ones! Bean bag cats, that is (we have just two real cats in the house). Some of my favorite bean bags are cats, especially Cheshire Cat, Cat in the Hat and the Hello Kitty, all of which have an emotional tie to my childhood. I loved "Alice in Wonderland," Dr. Seuss cartoons and all the Hello Kitty merchandise that was available when I was a youngster. For bean bag/cat lovers, there are plenty of excellent Ty Beanie Baby and Attic Treasures cats, as well as cartoon cats like Felix and Garfield.

Disney Aristocats: Duchess V1, Duchess V2, Marie V1, Marie V2.

Aristocats

From the Disney movie "Aristocats" come bean bags of Duchess and Marie. Part of the Disney Mini Bean Bag Plush collection, both came in two slightly different variations. (FYI: "Aristocats" was originally released in 1970. Eva Gabor was the voice of Duchess.)

Cat	Price Range
Duchess, V1, with whiskers	$12-$16
Duchess, V2, without whiskers	$7-$8
Marie, V1, 7 inches, lighter pink bows	$7-$8
Marie, V2, 8 inches, darker pink bows	$7-$8

Baby Boyds

Cat from the Baby Boyds line.

Cat	Price Range
Allie Fuzzbucket	$6-$8

Baby Boyds Allie Fuzzbucket.

Beanie Kids Floppy the cat.

Beanie Kids

Three cute cats in the Beanie Kids line.

Cat	Price Range
Floppy the cat (R)	$14-$18
Rusty the cat (R)	$10-$14
Tuffy the cat (R)	$10-$14

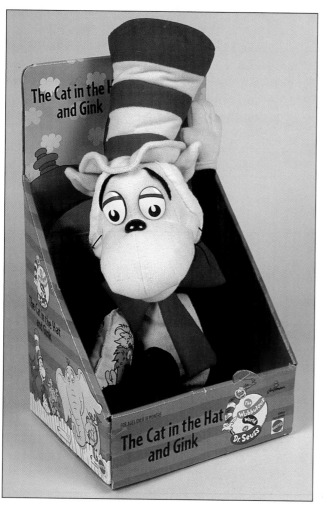

Mattel's Cat in the Hat.

The Cat in the Hat

From Dr. Seuss, The Cat in the Hat has found himself in two different bean bag sets: one by Mattel and one exclusively from Universal Studios "Islands of Adventure."

Cat	Price Range
The Cat in the Hat, Mattel	$9-$12
The Cat in the Hat, Universal "Island"	$9-$12

Catbert

Catbert is one of the most popular characters from the Dilbert set produced by Gund.

Cat	Price Range
Catbert	$8-$10

Catbert.

Cheshire Cat

From the 1951 Disney classic "Alice in Wonderland," are two great Cheshire Cat bean bags (part of the Disney Mini Bean Bag Plush collection). The Cheshire Cat Tea Cup bean bag is only available at Disneyland.

Cat	Price Range
Cheshire Cat	$8-$10
Cheshire Cat Tea Cup	$10-$12

Disney: Cheshire Cat Tea Cup and regular Cheshire Cat.

Felix the Cat

The old-time favorite cartoon character Felix the Cat has been made into a couple of excellent bean bags by A&A Plush.

Cat	Price Range
Felix	$10-$12
Felix, Valentine's, heart sewn on chest	$12-$15

Felix the Cat Valentine's and regular Felix the Cat.

Disney's Figaro.

Figaro

This cat is from the 1940 Disney classic "Pinocchio." "Pinocchio" fact: Won an Academy Award for best song ("When You Wish Upon a Star").

Cat	Price Range
Disney Mini Bean Bag Plush	
Figaro (R)	$7-$9
Star Beans (Mattel)	
Figaro	$5-$6

Nermal, Garfield and Arlene.

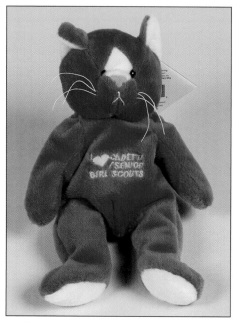

Cadet Girl Scout Cat.

Garfield Bean Bags

High quality bean bags of this famous cartoon feline and friends. These are available in the "Garfield Stuff" catalog (888-374-PAWS) or online at: www.catalog.garfield.com. If you're a Garfield enthusiast, check out the main Garfield website at: www.garfield.com.

Cat	Price Range
Arlene	$8-$10
Garfield	$8-$10
Nermal	$8-$10

Girl Scouts

Cat from the Belly Beans Girl Scout bean bags set by Mary Meyer.

Cat	Price Range
Cadet Girl Scout Cat	$8-$10

Various styles of Hello Kitty.

Mother Goose's Cat and the Fiddle..

Mother Goose
Cat & the Fiddle

An exclusive at Target stores in 1999.

Cat	Price Range
Cat and the Fiddle	$5-$8

Petco

Petco issued a cat and dog set of "Pet Pals" bean bags.

Cat	Price Range
Blue Mews cat	$5-$7
Holiday Mews cat	$6-$9

Hello Kitty

Find this old-time (1975) favorite online at *www.sanrio.com* for stores carrying these bean bags.

Cat	Price Range
Hello Kitty, bumblebee outfit	$6-$8
Hello Kitty, bunny suit, pink	$12-$15
Hello Kitty, bunny suit, purple	$14-$18
Hello Kitty, butterfly outfit	$7-$10
Hello Kitty, green suit	$6-$8
Hello Kitty, Hawaii	$7-$10
Hello Kitty, jester	$12-$14
Hello Kitty, mermaid outfit	$8-$10
Hello Kitty, pink suit	$8-$10
Hello Kitty, red suit	$6-$8
Hello Kitty, Santa suit	$12-$15
Hello Kitty, strawberry suit	$8-$10

Petco Blue Mews and Holiday Mews.

Pound Kitties.

Pussyfoot

This cute cartoon cat, always running from Pepe LePew, was issued by Warner Brothers Studio Stores.

Cat	Price Range
Pussyfoot (R)	$9-$11

Baby Sylvester (Warner Brothers), Baby Sylvester (Play-By-Play).

Warner Brothers: Birthday Sylvester, regular Sylvester and Santa Sylvester.

Pound Kitties

Mary Meyer produced a set of two Pound Kitties that go with two Pound Puppies. As with all Mary Meyer items, these are top-notch. They are available at finer gift shops.

Cat	Price Range
Orange Kitty	$7-$9
White Kitty	$7-$9

Warner Brother's Pussyfoot.

Sylvester the Cat

One version of Baby Sylvester is made by Play-By-Play; the other Baby Sylvester, along with the rest of the Sylvesters, are part of the Warner Brothers Studio Store Bean Bags line.

Cat	Price Range
Baby Sylvester (Play-By-Play)	$4-$6
Baby Sylvester (Warner Brothers)	$7-$9
Sylvester	$7-$9
Sylvester, Birthday	$7-$9
Sylvester, Halloween, 1999 (R)	$7-$9
Sylvester, Millennium 2000 (R)	$7-$9
Sylvester, Pilgrim, 1999 (R)	$7-$9
Sylvester, Santa, 1998 (R)	$9-$11
Sylvester, Santa with book, 1999	$7-$9
Sylvester, Talking	$8-$10

Tom the Cat

Tom the Cat, from the popular cartoon Tom & Jerry, has been made into bean bags twice: once by Chosun International with Cartoon Network tags, and the other is part of the Warner Brothers Studio Store Bean Bags line. The Cartoon Network version was available at Target stores in 1998 and might be retired.

Tom the cat (Cartoon Network) ....$9-$11
Tom (Warner Brothers) ....$7-$9

Tom (Cartoon Network) and Tom (Warner Brothers).

Ty Beanie Baby® Cats

Cats have been one of the traditionally strong issues in Ty's Beanie Baby line. For a while, it appeared that all the cats would rhyme with "ip," as in Snip, Chip, Flip, Zip, Nip, etc., it didn't continue as Pounce and Prance were released in 1998. Cats marked with an asterisk (*) after "Current" were due to retire by Dec. 31, 1999, according to a statement by Ty Inc.

Amber.

Chip.

Amber the gold tabby (R)

Style No. 4243	Born: Feb. 21, 1999
Rel: April 20, 1999	Retired: Dec. 31, 1999
Tag	**Price Range**
5th ....$6-$8	

Chip the cat (R)

Style No. 4121	Born: Jan. 26, 1997
Rel: May 11, 1997	Ret: March 31, 1999
Tag	**Price Range**
4th ....$10-$12	
5th ....$8-$10	

Flip the cat (R)

Style No. 4012	Born: Feb. 28, 1995
Released: 1996	Retired: Sept. 30, 1997
Tag	**Price Range**
3rd ....$55-$75	
4th ....$24-$32	

Nip, Version 3.

Nip the cat (R)

Style No. 4003   Born: March 6, 1994
Released: 1995   Retired: March 31, 1997

1st version: white face, belly

2nd version: all gold

3rd version: gold face, white paws

Version-Tag	Price Range
1-2nd	$350-$400
1-3rd	$275-$325
2-3rd	$700-$800
3-3rd	$125-$160
3-4th	$12-$16
3-5th	$10-$15

Pounce the cat (R)

Style No. 4122   Born: Aug. 28, 1997
Released: Dec. 31, 1997   Retired: March 31, 1999

Tag	Price Range
5th	$7-$8

Pounce.

Prance.

Prance the cat (R)

Style No. 4123   Born: Nov. 20, 1997
Released: Dec. 31, 1997   Retired: March 31, 1999

Tag	Price Range
5th	$7-$8

Scat the cat (R)

Style No. 4231   Born: May 27, 1998
Released: Dec. 31, 1998 Current*

Tag	**Price Range**
5th ....$6-$7	

Scat.

Silver.

Silver the gray tabby (R)

Style No. 4242   Born: Feb. 11, 1999
Released: April 21, 1999 Current*

Tag	**Price Range**
5th ....$8-$10	

Snip the cat (R)

Style No. 4120   Born: Oct. 22, 1996
Released: Jan. 1, 1997   Retired: Dec. 31, 1998

Tag	**Price Range**
4th ....$6-$8	
5th ....$6-$8	

Snip.

Zip (from left): Version 3 and Version 1.

Zip the cat (R)

Style No. 4004   Born: March 28, 1994
Released: 1995   Retired: May 1, 1998
1st version: white face and belly
2nd version: all black with pink ears
3rd version: white paws

Version-Tag	Price Range
1-2nd	$425-$525
1-3rd	$400-$475
2-3rd	$850-$975
3-3rd	$150-$175
3-4th	$15-$20
3-5th	$15-$20

Teenie Beanie Baby® Cats (McDonald's)

Just two cats so far in the three Teenie Beanie Baby promotions.

Tag	Price Range
Zip the cat, 1998	$3-$5
Chip the cat, 1999	$2-$4

Ty Beanie Buddy Cat

One cat in Ty's "Buddy" line.

Tag	Price Range
Chip the cat	$12-$16

Teenie Beanie Babies: Chip and Zip.

Ty Attic Treasures® Cats

Cats are one of the more-often used animals in the Ty Attic Treasures line. Some hard-to-find variations exist for some of the early cats.

Amethyst (R)

Retired: 1998

Hang tag/attire	**Price Range**
6th, light purple satin jumper ....$8-$12	

Amethyst.

Ebony, 15-inch version.

Ebony (R)

15-inch retired: 1997

13-inch retired: 1998

Hang tag/attire	**Price Range**
5th, 15-inch, maroon satin jumper.....................$8-$12	
6th, 13-inch, maroon satin jumper.....................$7-$10	

Katrina

Ivory (R)

Retired: 1997

Hang tag/attire   **Price Range**
5th, blue corduroy overalls ....$15-$20

Katrina (R)

Current

Hang tag/attire   **Price Range**
7th, green satin jumper...$5-$6

Ivory.

Pouncer (R)

Current

Hang tag/attire	Price Range
1st, both ears same color, red ribbon	$100-$150
1st, ears different colors, red ribbon	$100-$150
3rd, ears different colors, red ribbon	$60-$80
5th, green sweater	$6-$8
6th, peach satin jumper	$5-$6
7th, peach satin jumper	$5-$6

Pouncer in green sweater.

Pouncer in peach satin jumper.

Purrcy in green overalls.

Purrcy (R)

Current

Hang tag/attire	Price Range
2nd, pink ribbon	$100-$130
3rd, pink ribbon	$60-$80
5th, green sweater with gold buttons	$7-$10
5th, green sweater	$6-$8
6th, purple satin jumper	$5-$6
7th, purple satin jumper	$5-$6

Purrcy in purple satin jumper.

Whiskers (R)

Retired: Aug. 2, 1999

Hang tag/attire	Price Range
1st, both ears same color, pink ribbon	$100-$150
1st, ears different colors, pink ribbon	$100-$150
5th, maroon overalls	$6-$8
6th, blue satin jumper	$5-$6
7th, blue satin jumper	$5-$6

Whiskers in maroon overalls.

Whiskers in blue satin jumper.

The Dogs

Dogs are man's (and woman's) best friend. Well, actually diamonds are a woman's best friend, but I digress. Dogs can also be the best friend to a bean bag collector who loves to collect these canines. My husband's favorite is Scooby-Doo. My favorites are those from the Disney Mini Bean Bag Plush collection, such as "101 Dalmatians" and "Lady and the Tramp." If you haven't seen the Hush Puppies bean bags, I suggest you do. These are some of the best advertising bean bags you'll ever see. Another advertising character to get your hands on is Buster Brown's dog Tige (if you were wondering, it is *Tige* and not *Tiger*). Ty weighs in big with plenty of dogs in its Beanie Baby line.

Disney (top) Cruella De Vil, Jewel; (middle) 101 Pup V1, 101 Pup V2, 101 Pup V3, Lucky V2; (bottom) Lucky V3, Lucky V.

101 Dalmatians

Disney's "101 Dalmatians" premiered in 1961. It has gone on to become one of the most beloved Disney films of all time. The Disney Mini Bean Bag Plush is excellent and extensive. The four Mattel Star Beans pups were available exclusively through an offer on the "101 Dalmatians" video. *"101 Dalmatians" fact:* This film cost $4 million to make!

<u>Dog</u>	<u>Price Range</u>
Disney Mini Bean Bag Plush	
101 Dalmatians Pup, test, "V" on forehead, no spots on belly (R)	$25-$35
101 Dalmatians Pup, V2, no "V" on forehead, spots on belly (R)	$12-$14
101 Dalmatians Pup, V3 "V" on forehead, spots on belly	$9-$12
Jewel	$8-$10
Lucky, France exclusive, red collar	$12-$15
Lucky, V1, no "V" on forehead, larger head, $9 or $10 sticker	$12-$14
Lucky, V2, "V" on forehead	$12-$16
Lucky, V3, no "V" on forehead, smaller head, no $9 sticker	$6-$8
Lucky, Sound	$7-$9

Patch , France exclusive, green collar ....$12-$16
Penny, France exclusive, pink collar ....$12-$16
Penny, Sound ....$7-$9

Star Beans (Mattel)
Freckles ....$9-$11
Patch ....$9-$11
Penny ....$9-$11
Pepper ....$9-$11

Disney France-exclusives (from left): Lucky, Patch and Penny.

Star Beans (from left): Pepper, Penny and Freckles.

An All Dog's Christmas

These two bean bags are from a Denny's 1998 holiday promotion for the movie "An All Dog's Christmas Carol." The animated movie featured the voices of Dom DeLuise, Sheena Easton, Charles Nelson Reilly and Bebe Neuwirth.

Dog	Price Range
Itchy	$5-$6
Scratchy	$5-$6

Baby Boyds

Pair of dogs from the Baby Boyds line.

Dog	Price Range
Barkley McFarkle	$6-$8
Bunky McFarkle	$6-$8

Baby Boyds: Barkley McFarkle.

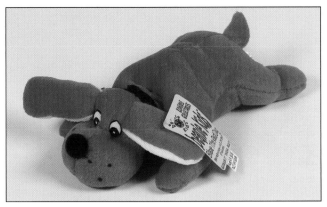

Beanie Kids Blaze.

Beanie Kids

A total of seven dogs, some very scarce, so far in the Beanie Kids line.

Dog	Price Range
Blaze the dog (R)	$55-$70
Rover the red nose reindog (R)	$7-$9
Spike the bullie	$7-$9
Spot the dog	$6-$8
Sunny the dog (R)	$45-$60
Tango the dog (R)	$90-$110
Woof the dog, talking (R)	$9-$12

Blue's Clues Blue bean bags and Magenta bean bag.

Blue's Clues

Highly popular Nickelodeon kid's program has sprouted three bean bags so far.

Dog	Price Range
Blockbuster Video Blue	$7-$10
Blockbuster Video Magenta	$8-$11
Mott's Blue (with birthday hat)	$8-$10

Bob Evans Restaurant

From Bob Evans Restaurant, a regional eatery.

Dog	Price Range
Biscuit	$6
Gravy	$6

Bob Evans Restaurant: Biscuit and Gravy.

Buster Brown's Tige.

Buster Brown's Tige

Reportedly, Tige was available as an in-store premium at Buster Brown outlets and is retired. This is an excellent bean bag with a lot of collectibility.

Dog	Price Range
Tige	$10-$14

Cartoon Dogs

Several cartoons have had dogs as the main characters. As with almost all cartoon characters, these translate well into bean bag form.

Dog	Price Range
Cartoon Network	
Droopy	$5-$7
Huckleberry Hound	$5-$7
Oscar Mayer	
Dino	$8-$10

Cartoon Network Droopy (left) and WB Droopy (right).

Oscar-Mayer Dino.

Huckleberry Hound: The two on the left are Cartoon Network versions, while the one on the right is from Warner Brothers.

WB regular K-9 and Christmas K-9.

Warner Brothers Studio Store Bean Bags

Dog	Price Range
Augie Doggie(R)	$6-$8
Astro (R)	$7-$9
Dino (R)	$8-$10
Droopy	$6-$8
Dum Dum (R)	$6-$8
Hardy Har Har (R)	$6-$8
Hong Kong Phooey (R)	$8-$11
Huckleberry Hound (R)	$7-$9
K-9	$6-$8
K-9, Christmas LE	$7-$10
Marc Antony (R)	$7-$10
Mutley	$6-$8

From left: WB Dum Dum, Hong Kong Phooey, Marc Antony and Mutley.

Clifford the Big Red Dog.

Clifford the Big Red Dog

Scholastic has featured some children's characters as bean bags.

Dog	Price Range
Clifford the Big Red Dog	$9-$12

Disney Dogs

Here are some of the dogs featured in Disney films that are a part of the Disney Mini Bean Bag line. (Also see "101 Dalmatians," "Lady and the Tramp" and "Pluto.")

Dog	Price Range
"Mulan"	
Lil' Brother	$6-$8
Lil' Brother, Sound	$6-$8

Oliver and Dodger from Oliver & Co.

Mulan: Lil' Brother.

"Oliver & Co."	
Dodger	$6-$8
Oliver	$6-$8
"Peter Pan"	
Nana	$6-$8

Dogbert

Dogbert is from the Dilbert set produced by Gund.

Cat	Price Range
Dogbert	$8-$10

Dilbert's Dogbert.

Pooka from "Anastasia."

Dole Pooka (Anastasia)

Pooka, a dog from the animated film "Anastasia" was available as a premium through Dole.

Dog	Price Range
Pooka (R)	$6

"Dr. Dolittle" press kit bean bags.

Dr. Dolittle Movie

A pair of small bean bags were issued as part of the press kit for the 1998 film "Dr. Dolittle," starring Eddie Murphy. The entire kit consists of these bean bags, a water bowl and a pair of pins.

Dog	Price Range
Jake the tiger	$4-$6
Lucky the Dog	$4-$6

Flavorite's Riley bean bag.

Flavorite

Riley is a premium bean bag from Flavorite Cereal.

Dog	Price Range
Riley the dog	$8

Pete from The Little Rascals.

For Pete's Sake

Pete, the dog from "The Little Rascals" shows, was a bean bag premium for buying the movie "For Pete's Sake."

Dog	Price Range
Pete	$18-$22

Odie from Garfield.

Garfield's Odie

Garfield's dog nemesis Odie was made into a nice bean bag.

Dog	Price Range
Odie	$8-$10

Girl Scouts

Dog from the Belly Beans Girl Scout bean bags set by Mary Meyer.

Dog	Price Range
Junior Girl Scout Dog	$8-$10

Junior Girl Scout Dog.

Harley-Davidson's Spike.

Harley-Davidson Bean Bag Plush

The Harley-Davidson Bean Bag Plush characters, first released in 1997, are still proving popular sellers in the Harley and bean bag collecting communities. Three dogs have been issued so far. Made by Cavanagh.

Dog	Price Range
Spike bulldog	$6-$8
Tanker bulldog	$6-$8
Thunder bulldog	$6-$8

Hush Puppies Bean Bags

The Applause Hush Puppies dog bean bag sets are some of the best ever issued.

Dog	Price Range
Applause Set #1 (R)	
Beet	$8-$10
Blue Bayou	$8-$10
Logo Basset	$8-$10
Miami Coral	$8-$10
Royal Purple	$8-$10
Salad Green	$8-$10
Applause Set #2 (R)	
Berry Frappe	$6-$8

Dog	Price Range
Bunting Blue	$6-$8
Chantilly	$6-$8
Jet Black	$6-$8
Logo Basset	$6-$8
Applause Set #3 (R)	
Cascade Blue	$6-$8
Lemon Meringue	$6-$8
Lively Lilac	$6-$8
Meadow Mist	$6-$8
Spring Logo	$6-$8
Passion Pink	$6-$8

Hush Puppies set #1.

Dog	Price Range
Applause Scented	
Lilac, scented	$8-$10
Meadow Mist, scented	$8-$10
Classic Merchandising	
Brown and white dog, laying down	$8-$10

Hush Puppies set #3.

Hush Puppies set #2.

Lady and the Tramp

This 1955 classic has seen several dog bean bags released in the Disney Mini Bean Bag Plush line.

Lady V2.

Dog	Price Range
Disney Mini Bean Bag Plush	
Jock	$6-$8
Lady, V1, red collar	$6-$8
Lady, V2, blue collar, UK exclusive w/video	$16-$22
Tramp, V1, brown collar	$6-$8
Tramp, V2, reddish-brown collar, slightly smaller	$6-$8
Trusty	$6-$8

Trusty, Lady V1, Tramp V1, Tramp V2 and Jock.

Old Navy

Lucky the dog bean bags are available at Old Navy outlet stores. Well made and worth getting.

Dog	Price Range
Lucky, Easter bunny suit	$10-$12
Lucky, flowers	$6-$8
Lucky, Fourth of July, hat and T-shirt	$6-$8
Lucky, Old Navy T-shirt	$6-$8
Lucky, Old Navy scarf	$6-$8

Old Navy: Lucky with flowers and Lucky with Old Navy T-shirt.

Disney Pluto: (top, from left) test, V2, V3; (bottom) Reindeer, Tomorrowland.

Pluto

Pluto is the favorite character of many Disney collectors. He's been included in several lines of bean bags. Pluto fact: Pluto starred in 48 of his own cartoons, plus those with Mickey, Donald and others.

Dog	Price Range
Disney Mini Bean Bag Plush	
Pluto, Reindeer, LE 1997	$16-$21
Pluto, test, tag says 9", longer ears, footpads on hind feet (R)	$20-$24
Pluto, Tomorrowland (R)	$7-$9
Pluto, V2, tag has no measurement, no footpads (R)	$6-$8
Pluto, V3, plastic eyes, more plush (R)	$6-$8
Mickey for Kids Bean Bags (Mattel)	
Pluto	$5-$6
Star Beans (Mattel)	
Pluto	$5-$6

Pound Puppies

Mary Meyer set of two Pound Puppies bean bags (that go along with the pair of Pound Kitties). Very cute.

Dog	Price Range
Black Dog	$7-$9
Tan Dog	$7-$9

Pound Puppies bean bags.

RCA Chipper.

RCA Chipper

Chipper is the puppy to the famous RCA dog Nipper. Reportedly, the Chipper bean bag was made as an employee program incentive.

Dog	Price Range
Chipper	$12-$16

Scooby-Doo

Scooby-Doo is likely the best-loved cartoon dog of all time, and 1999 marked the 30th anniversary of the first Scooby cartoon. Already, Scooby has had many different bean bags, and the most collectible ones are from Warner Brothers. The WB Scoobys are definitely the coolest! The four Scoobys in the K-mart set were available in the spring of 1999 with the purchase of a Scooby-Doo T-shirt (these are probably pretty scarce). The Cartoon Network Scooby was sold in Target stores in 1997-98. The Oscar-Meyer Scooby is similar to the Cartoon Network version, and was a mail-in offer that didn't receive mass distribution.

Dog	Price Range
Cartoon Network	
Scooby-Doo	$10-$14

Dog	Price Range
K-mart	
Scooby, sitting, pink tie-dye shirt	$8-$12

WB: I Love New York, Home Run and Surfer.

	Price Range
Scooby, sitting, purple tie-dye shirt	$8-$12
Scooby, standing, flowered shorts	$8-$12
Scooby, standing, tie-dye shorts	$8-$12
Oscar Mayer	
Scooby	$12-$16
Warner Brothers Studio Store Bean Bags	
Scooby-Doo, Antlers, 1998 (R)	$12-$14
Scooby-Doo, Atlantic City	$12-$14
Scooby-Doo, Baseball (Father's Day), V1: no freckles on chin	$9-$12
Scooby-Doo, Baseball (Father's Day), V2: freckles on chin	$9-$12
Scooby-Doo, Bath floater	$9-$12
Scooby-Doo, Beau Rivage	n/a
Scooby-Doo, Birthday	$9-$12
Scooby-Doo, Chicago	$10-$12
Scooby-Doo, Graduate (R)	$12-$15
Scooby-Doo, Easter 1998 (R)	$30-$40
Scooby-Doo, Easter 1999 (R)	$10-$12
Scooby-Doo, Hawaii, Hawaii exclusive	$12-$14
Scooby-Doo, Home Run	$8-$10
Scooby-Doo, I Love New York, NY exclusive	$10-$12
Scooby-Doo, It's a Boy	$7-$10
Scooby-Doo, Lake Tahoe	n/a
Scooby-Doo, Millennium 2000 (R)	$8-$10
Scooby-Doo, Nutcracker, 1998 (R)	$9-$12
Scooby-Doo, Pilgrim, 1999 (R)	$9-$12
Scooby-Doo, Reindeer, 1997 (R)	$150-$175
Scooby-Doo, Roman, Las Vegas exclusive	$9-$12
Scooby-Doo, Snowman, 1999 (catalog exclusive) (R)	$12-$15
Scooby-Doo, Surfboard (R)	$7-$9
Scooby-Doo, Talking	$9-$12
Scooby-Doo, Thanksgiving, 1999	$7-$9

Scooby-Doo, T-shirt (Atlantic City) ....$12-$15
Scooby-Doo, T-shirt (Boston) ....$12-$15
Scooby-Doo, T-shirt (Chicago) ....$9-$12
Scooby-Doo, T-shirt (Lake Tahoe) ....$12-$15
Scooby-Doo, T-shirt (Miami) ....$12-$15
Scooby-Doo, T-shirt (Orlando) ....$9-$12

Scooby-Doo, V1: "S" on collar ....$25-$30
Scooby-Doo, V2: "SD" on collar ....$6-$8
Scooby-Doo, Vampire, 1998 (R) ....$12-$15
Scooby-Doo, Witch, 1999 (R) ....$10-$12
Scrappy-Doo ....$6-$8

WB: (front) Baseball V1, Baseball V2; (back) V1, V2, I Love NY.

Cartoon Network Scooby.

WB: Roman (Las Vegas) and Easter 1999.

WB: (front) Easter 1998, Reindeer; (back) Antlers, Nutcracker, Vampire.

WB: Hawaii (Hawaii exclusive), Home Run and Surfboard.

Sesame Street Beans

Barkley is the lone dog on Sesame Street and the lone dog in Tyco's Sesame Street Beans set.

Dog	Price Range
Barkley	$6-$8

Sesame Street Beans Barkley.

Snoopy

Several Peanuts bean bag sets are heavy in Snoopy!

Dog	Price Range
Colorful Images (Applause)	
Snoopy	$5-$6
Snoopy, Santa	$5-$6
Peanuts Collection, Kohl's (Applause)	
Snoopy as Flying Ace	$6-$8
Snoopy as Joe Cool	$6-$8
Snoopy in pajamas	$6-$8
Snoopy & Friends (Irwin Toy)	
Snoopy	$3-$5
Snoopy as Flying Ace	$3-$5
Snoopy as Joe Cool	$3-$5

Colorful Images Snoopy and Santa Snoopy.

Three Snoopys from the Snoopy & Friends set.

Kohl's Peanuts Collection Snoopy trio.

Spike the Dog (Rugrats)

The highly popular Nickelodeon cartoon "Rugrats" has seen several sets of bean bags produced thus far, all of which include Spike the Dog.

Dog	Price Range
Spike the dog, Applause	$3-$4
Spike, Blockbuster exclusive	$4-$6
Spike the dog, Mattel Christmas	$6-$8

Spike, from left: Mattel Christmas, Blockbuster and Applause.

Toto (Wizard of Oz)

"And we'll make a bean bag out of your little doggy, too!" Both Warner Brothers and Trevco made Wizard of Oz bean bag sets, and each included Dorothy's little dog Toto.

Dog	Price Range
Toto, Trevco Merry-O Collection	$5-$7
Toto, Warner Brothers	$7-$9

From left: WB Toto and Trevco Merry-O Collection Toto.

Ty Beanie Baby Dogs

Dogs are a strong area in Ty's Beanie Baby line. This will probably continue, as there are many breeds of dogs yet to become Beanie Babies. Dogs marked with an asterisk (*) after "Current" were due to retire by Dec. 31, 1999, according to a statement by Ty Inc.

Bones the dog.

Bones the dog (R)

Style No. 4001   Born: Jan. 18, 1994
Released: 1994   Retired: May 1, 1998

Tag	Price Range
1st	$200-$240
2nd	$125-$160
3rd	$50-$60
4th	$10-$12
5th	$10-$12

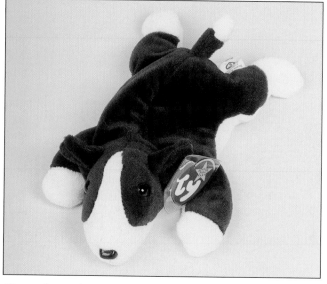

Bruno the terrier.

Bruno the terrier (R)

Style No. 4183   Born: Sept. 9, 1997
Released: Dec. 31, 1997   Retired: Sept. 18, 1998

Tag	Price Range
5th	$5-$7

Butch the bull terrier (R)

Style No. 4227
Released: Dec. 31, 1998

Born: Oct. 2, 1998
Retired: Dec. 31, 1999

Tag	Price Range
5th	$5-$7

Butch the bull terrier.

Doby the doberman.

Doby the doberman (R)

Style No. 4110
Released: Jan. 1, 1997

Born: Oct. 9, 1996
Retired: Dec. 31, 1998

Tag	Price Range
4th	$8-$10
5th	$8-$10

Dotty the dalmatian (R)

Style No. 4100
Released: May 11, 1997

Born: Oct. 17, 1996
Retired: Dec. 31, 1998

Tag	Price Range
4th	$8-$10
5th	$8-$10

Dotty and dalmatian.

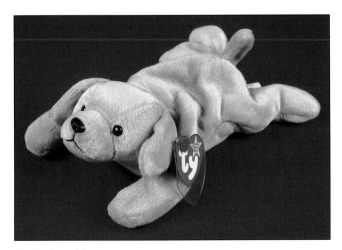

Fetch the golden retriever.

Fetch the golden retriever (R)

Style No. 4189
Released: May 31, 1998

Born: Feb. 4, 1997
Retired: Dec. 31, 1998

Tag	Price Range
5th	$10-$12

Gigi the poodle.

Luke the Lab (R)

Style No. 4214   Born: June 15, 1998
Released: Dec. 31-98   Current*

Tag	Price Range
5th	$8-$10

Nanook the husky.

Gigi the poodle (R)

Style No. 4191   Born: April 7, 1997
Released: May 31, 1998   Current*

Tag	Price Range
5th	$5-$7

Luke the Lab.

Nanook the husky (R)

Style No. 4104   Born: Nov. 21, 1996
Released: May 11, 1997   Retired: March 31, 1999

Tag	Price Range
4th	$8-$10
5th	$7-$9

Pugsley the pug dog (R)

Style No. 4106
Released: May 11, 1997

Born: May 2, 1996
Retired: March 31, 1999

Tag	Price Range
4th	$8-$10
5th	$7-$9

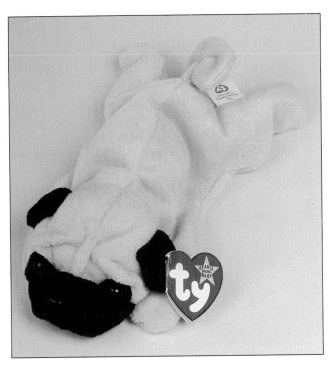

Pugsley the pug dog.

Rover the dog (R)

Style No. 4101
Released: 1996

Born: May 30, 1996
Retired: May 1, 1998

Tag	Price Range
4th	$15-$20
5th	$15-$20

Rover the dog.

Scottie the dog.

Scottie the Dog (R)

Style No. 4102
Released: 1996

Born: June 15, 1996
Retired: May 1, 1998

Tag	Price Range
4th	$15-$20
5th	$15-$20

Sparky the dalmatian.

Sparky the dalmatian (R)

Style No. 4100   Born: Feb. 27, 1996
Released: 1996   Retired: May 11, 1997

Tag	**Price Range**
4th	$75-$90

Spot the dog (R)

Style No. 4000   Born: Jan. 3, 1993
Released: 1994   Retired: Sept. 30, 1997

1st version: no spot on back

2nd version: spot on back

Version-Tag	**Price Range**
1-1st	$1,700-$1,900
1-2nd	$1,500-$1,700
2-2nd	$350-$450
2-3rd	$145-$170
2-4th	$35-$45

Spot the dog, with spot.

Spunky the cocker spaniel (R)

Style No. 4184   Born: Jan. 14, 1997
Released: Dec. 31, 1997   Retired: March 31, 1999

Tag	**Price Range**
5th	$8-$10

Spunky the cocker spaniel.

Tiny the chihuahua (R)

Style No. 4234   Born: 9-8-98
Released: Dec. 31-98   Current*

Tag   **Price Range**
5th ....$8-$10

Tiny the chihuahua.

Tracker the basset hound.

Tracker the basset hound (R)

Style No. 4198   Born: June 5, 1997
Released: May 31, 1998   Retired: Dec. 31, 1999

Tag   **Price Range**
5th ....$8-$10

Tuffy the terrier (R)

Style No. 4108   Born: Oct. 12, 1996
Released: May 11, 1997   Retired: Dec. 31, 1998

Tag   **Price Range**
4th ....$8-$10
5th ....$8-$10

Tuffy the terrier.

Weenie the dachshund.

Weenie the dachshund (R)

Style No. 4013	Born: July 20, 1995
Released: 1996	Retired: May 1, 1998

Tag	Price Range
3rd	$90-$115
4th	$20-$25
5th	$18-$24

Wrinkles the bulldog (R)

Style No. 4103	Born: May 1, 1996
Released: 1996	Retired: Sept. 22, 1998

Tag	Price Range
4th	$8-$10
5th	$8-$10

Wrinkles the bulldog.

Sports Events Beanie Baby Dogs

Baseball

Atlanta Braves, Pugsley.

Dog	Price Range
1998	
Atlanta Braves, Pugsley, 9-2-98	$20-$30
Cincinnati Reds, Rover, 8-16-98	$20-$30
New York Yankees, Bones, 3-10-98	$35-$50
San Francisco Giants, Tuffy, 8-30-98	$20-$30
Tampa Bay Devil Rays, Weenie, 6-26-98	$20-$30
Texas Rangers, Pugsley, 8-4-98	$20-$30
1999	
Houston Astros, Tiny, 7-18-99	$15-$25
Texas Rangers, Luke, 9-5-99	$15-$25

Teenie Beanie Baby® Dogs

Four Teenie Bean Baby dogs were issued in the last two promotions.

Dog	Price Range
Bones the dog, 1998	$3-$4
Doby the doberman, 1998	$4-$6
'Nook the husky, 1999	$2-$4
Spunky the cocker spaniel, 1999	$2-$4

Teenie Beanie Babies Bones and Doby.

Ty Attic Treasures® Dogs

There are not a lot of dogs in the Attic Treasures line, but there are some nice ones.

Brewster (R)

Retired: 1997

Hang tag/attire	Price Range
2nd, light blue overalls, buttons	$50-$60
3rd, light blue overalls, buttons	$40-$50
4th, light blue overalls	$30-$40
5th, light blue overalls	$15-$18

Murphy (R)

Retired: 1997

Hang tag/attire	Price Range
2nd, overalls, buttons	$45-$55
3rd, overalls	$35-$45
4th, overalls, buttons	$25-$35
5th, overalls	$15-$18

Murphy.

Brewster with and without buttons.

Scooter.

Scooter (R)

Retired: 1997

Hang tag/attire	Price Range
2nd, sweater	$70-$90
5th, sweater	$35-$50

Scruffy.

Scruffy (R)

Retired: 1999

Hang tag/attire	Price Range
6th	$5-$7
7th	$5-$7

Spencer (R)

Retired: 1997

Hang tag/attire	Price Range
5th, sweater	$22-$28
5th, overalls	$15-$18

Spencer.

Tracy (R)

Retired: 1997

Hang tag/attire	Price Range
5th, overalls	$22-$28

Tracy.

VFW Buddy Poppy.

VFW Buddy Poppy

Available through the VFW, Poppy is currently sold out, but more will possibly be distributed this year.

Dog	**Price Range**
Buddy Poppy	$7-$10

Wishbone bean bags.

Wishbone

Denny's promotion included two Wishbone (PBS) dogs bean bags. The Dr. Jeckyl and Equity toy versions were available at convenience and mass market stores.

Dog	**Price Range**
Wishbone, Dr. Jeckyl	$5-$7
Wishbone, Denny's, laying down	$6-$8
Wishbone, Denny's, sitting	$6-$8
Wishbone, Equity Toys, laying down	$4-$6